Samuel Felton

Gleanings on Gardens

Chiefly respecting those of the ancient style in England

Samuel Felton

Gleanings on Gardens
Chiefly respecting those of the ancient style in England

ISBN/EAN: 9783337070144

Printed in Europe, USA, Canada, Australia, Japan

Cover: Foto ©Lupo / pixelio.de

More available books at **www.hansebooks.com**

This work was originally published in 1829, *and copies of the Edition of that date are now very rarely met with. In this reprint some revision of the original issue has been attempted, though certain quaint and curious forms of spelling remain as in the original. A Bibliography of the books referred to casually throughout the work, and an Index of Names, &c., have been added.*

GLEANINGS ON GARDENS

CHIEFLY RESPECTING THOSE OF THE ANCIENT STYLE IN ENGLAND

By S. FELTON

PRIVATELY PRINTED FOR
ARTHUR L. HUMPHREYS
187 PICCADILLY, LONDON
1897

PREFACE.

MY inducement for publishing the following pages is, in one instance, by way of answer to many requests that have been made to me on account of what the conductor of the *Gardener's Magazine* subjoined to a short communication I sent to him in 1826; and which communication, and its answer, appeared in that Magazine for October, 1826. I have given them below.* I beg, therefore, to say

---

* 'SIR,—If the three underwritten brief suggestions are worthy of your acceptance, or if they will be the means of inducing any person to effect something of the same kind, they are at your service.

'I am, Sir, your constant reader,

'*June,* 1826.   'S. FELTON.'

'1. Would it be desirable to have *A Catalogue Raisonné of Books on Horticulture,* English and foreign ?—The first series of the English catalogue to be brought down to the demise of Henry VIII.; the second to that of Charles II.; the third to that of George II.; the fourth to that of George III.

'Nearly fifty years ago, I saw in the libraries at Caen and

that it is not in my power, for many reasons (declining health being one), to supply any of the *desiderata* there alluded to. The *Catalogue Raisonné*, as well as the *Biography of some early Horticulturists*, would find, we all know, abundant materials towards composing them in many rich pages in the *Encyclopædia of Gardening*, and in the libraries of Oxford, Cambridge, the British Museum, in those of the late Sir Joseph Banks, and of the present W. Forsyth, Esq., and in those of the London, Caledonian, and other

Rouen, several Anglo-Norman MSS. on the cultivation of cider, and on general agriculture, and very possibly there may be some concerning horticulture. Many libraries on the Continent, no doubt, will throw light on this subject, particularly those of Ghent, Bruges, Brussels, and Holland.

'2. A curious work might be formed by giving copies of some of those plates which adorn many old books which contain descriptions of some of our *Old English Gardens*, belonging to our ancient religious houses, or to the mansions of our old nobility and gentry. Some of these plates are by admirable foreign engravers. They might be classed under each county, and brought down to the demise of George II.

'Ray dedicates his *Flora* to Lady Gerrard, of Gerrard's Bromley, in Staffordshire. Plot gives a plate of this mansion, and part of its garden. See also the garden in Vertue's fine whole-length print of Sir P. Sydney. Perhaps there may be somewhere a plate of Sir W. Raleigh's garden at Sherborne, in Dorsetshire. We have this account of his house: "A most fyne house, beautified with

Horticultural Societies. I unwillingly relinquish this latter work, being certain that I could by no means do the subject justice. I have very slightly attempted it in a little tract, published a few months, ago under the title of *On the Portraits of English Authors on Gardening.* Both these subjects must diffuse in the mind of the composer nearly the same delight with which Horace Walpole prepared the papers of *Vertue;* which Dr. Pulteney no doubt experienced when sketching the *Progress of Botany;* which the Rev.

orchardes, gardens, and groves of such varietie and delyght, that whether you consider the goodnesse of soyle, the pleasauntnesse of the seate, and other delycacies belonging to it, it is unparalleled by any in these partes."

'What information, on this head, might have been gleaned from the late Sir W. Temple, or from Kent, or from even him who has immortalised Kent, from Mr. Pope himself, whose chief delight was in his own garden, or from Mr. Evelyn, Mr. Gray, Mr. Mason, or from Mr. Bates, the celebrated and ancient horticulturist of High Wycombe, who died there some few years ago, at the great age of eighty-nine!

'This work might include many scattered and curious gleanings from our old gardens. I will mention only one: "Talking of hedges," says Mr. Cobbett, in one of his *Rural Rides,* "reminds me of having seen a box-hedge just as I came out of Petworth, more than twelve feet broad, and about fifteen feet high. I daresay it is several centuries old. I think it is about forty yards long. It is a great curiosity." In some of the villages near Northampton, are

Patrick Keith must have felt when composing the Introduction to his *System of Physiological Botany;* or which warmed the breast of Hector St. John, when dedicating his *Letters from an American Farmer* to the Abbé Raynal.

With respect to the plates of *our old English gardens*, I have only to say that when I published, in 1785, *Miscellanies on Ancient and Modern Gardening, and on the Scenery of Nature*, I formed a plan of publishing views of some secluded, curious old mansions,

some elder trees of singularly unusual size. About the year 1688, many gardens would then have furnished one with what is now suggested, if we may judge from what Worlidge then wrote: "Neither is there a noble or pleasant seat in England, but hath its gardens for pleasure and delight. So that we may, without vanity, conclude, that a garden of pleasant avenues, walks, fruits, flowers, grots, and other branches springing from it, well composed, is the only complete and permanent inanimate object of delight the world affords."

'3. *A Biography of some early Horticulturists* would diffuse much curious matter.'

'We should be much gratified if Mr. Felton would supply some of the above interesting desiderata himself. Though we have not the advantage of his acquaintance, and do not know his address, we can infer from his communication that few are so capable of instructing and entertaining the curious horticulturist. A biography of Mr. Bates, or any anecdotes respecting him, would very acceptable.'

such as those not generally known to the public, from their being more buried in the bosom of the country:

'*Et dont l'aspect imprime, et commande l'honneur.*'

With their venerable decorations of ancient splendour, their gardens, and their portraits; many of beauties whose cheeks 'bloom in after-ages,' and where I have indignantly seen many rich treasures of painting mouldering on their walls. What I then collected was, many years ago, destroyed or parted with; for those whom I most wished to have pleased have long since been shrouded in the silence of the tomb:

'*Each in his narrow cell for ever laid.*'

One viewed such neglected and venerable seats with regret at the decay of so many appendages of the grandeur, or happiness, of former times; one trod the ground where many eminent and worthy men resided with pensive emotions of respect (so Johnson felt when viewing the alcove and garden at Welwyn), and as the 'inaudible and noiseless foot of time' has long since extinguished these ancient and, some of them, magnificent houses, with their hospitable establishments, one can only reflect on what Madame de Sevigné says: 'La vie est courte, c'est bien tôt fait;

le fleuve qui nous entraine est si rapide, qu'à peine pouvons-nous y paroître.'

I cannot refrain from giving the following extract from Dr. Pulteney's *Sketches*, just premising that the writings of John Ray must impress every one with the highest sentiments of respect and veneration for that eminent man, whose whole life was devoted to charitable and benevolent purposes. 'It may gratify the curiosity of some,' says Dr. Pulteney, 'who reverence the name of Mr. Ray, to be informed, that in one of these excursions Dr. Watson was led, by his respect to the memory of that great and good man, to visit the spot where he had lived at Black Notley, in Essex. This was in the year 1760. To Dr. Watson this was classical ground. I was informed by him at that time that he found Mr. Ray's monument removed out of the church, where it formerly stood, into the churchyard, and hardly visible for brambles; these he had removed while he stayed. That he found the house in a state which indicated no alteration having taken place, except what more than half-a-century of time might be supposed necessarily to have occasioned; unless that indeed some of the windows were stopped up to save the tax; and that the orchard bore all the appearance of being, as near as possible, in the state in which it must have been in Mr. Ray's lifetime. That the inhabitants of the village knew little of him, and the people of the house had only heard that he was a great traveller.'

A writer whose name I forget observes, 'Where is now the Greek, or the Roman, or the Goth, or the Norman ?—all gone down and mingled with the mass of mankind. What imperial nation of antiquity has retained its laws, or religion, or countenance ? The grave has mixed them all in one great decay, and other masters of empire have marched upon the soil and trampled out their monuments.'

Not many years ago a rich illuminated pedigree of the ancient, but now forgotten and extinct, family of Cufaude was discovered stopping the broken casement of a miserable cottage at Basingstoke.*

The following article is from No. 311 of that amusing assemblage of literature, the *Mirror*: 'In the churchyard of Aldworth, near Newbury, is a yew-tree which, according to the best information, is not less than 800 years old. The girth of one part of the

---

* 'Here's a fine revolution if we had the trick to see it.'
Hamlet.

trunk is above nine yards, and its branches extend over the graves beneath to an immense extent. On entering the church we are struck with astonishment at the sight of the gigantic effigies and tombs that occupy a very large proportion of its interior; there are four reclining figures of men in armour, and on a tomb near the pulpit, in the middle of the church, are figures in brass of Nicholas, Lord de la Beche, and his lady, resting their heads on stone pillars, and their feet on lions or dogs. The effigies are all of the family of de la Beche, who came from Normandy with William the First. Tradition says there was a pedigree of the family formerly hung at the east end of the south aisle; but that, when Elizabeth visited Aldworth in one of her excursions, Leicester took it down to show to Her Majesty and it was never replaced. The arches against the north and south walls over the tomb of Lord and Lady de la Beche are much enriched with quartrefoils, roses, crocketts, &c., in the prevailing taste of Edward the Third.' These few instances feelingly remind one 'what shadows we are and what shadows we pursue.'

A translation from some Chinese book thus moralises on the revolutions of families: 'These verdant mountains, these lovely meadows, were once possessed by families now gone to decay. Let not the present possessors exult too much; others after them may be masters in their turn.'

I offer nearly all the following pages, meagre as they are, as a skeleton, or a very loose sketch, and in the hope that some spirited and affluent person may publish what I have in the first page of the following work suggested; and that such person may be induced to make application to the descendants of some of those families who may have preserved vestiges, or drawings, of gardens, which were once the pride and delight of their ancestors. That oil paintings of our ancient gardens now exist in the mansions of many of our nobility and gentry there can be no doubt. If such a work as the above proposed one should ever strike the mind of the author of the *Essay on the Life, Character, and Talents of Thomas Chatterton*, and whose rich plates so grandly exhibit that

'. . . . mysterie of a human hand,
The pride of Bristowe and the western land,'

there can be no doubt but that the engravings which would then be produced of our ancient gardens would deserve the same honest testimony which was paid to his other plates of our *Ancient Architecture and Cathedral Antiquities*, viz.: 'With respect to the plates, it would not be easy to find any language too emphatical in praise. Nothing more exquisite has been seen, or can be conceived, than the execution of them.'

CONTENTS.

CHAP.		PAGE
I.	GLEANINGS ON GARDENS, CHIEFLY RESPECTING THOSE OF THE ANCIENT STYLE IN ENGLAND	1
II.	DESCRIPTION OF MANY GARDENS IN ENGLAND AND SCOTLAND IN 1714	11
III.	ON CONVENTUAL GARDENS	57
IV.	ON GARDEN BURIAL	60
V.	ON COTTAGE GARDENS	73
VI.	ON THE CULTIVATION OF THE VINE IN ENGLAND	83
VII.	MR. POPE'S LETTER TO MARTHA BLOUNT, DESCRIBING THE SEAT OF SIR W. RALEIGH	88
VIII.	POPE'S VILLA AT TWICKENHAM	96
	BIBLIOGRAPHY	103
	INDEX	119

GLEANINGS ON GARDENS.

CHAPTER I.

GLEANINGS ON GARDENS, CHIEFLY RESPECTING THOSE OF THE ANCIENT STYLE IN ENGLAND.

IN that rich assemblage of whatever concerns horticulture, Loudon's *Encyclopædia of Gardening*, is (page 71) a beautiful plate of Chatsworth; and in the second volume of Britton's *Architectural Antiquities* are two fascinating plates, of the old garden at Oxnead Hall and of that at Longleat. The sight of these plates may, and I hope will, induce some gentleman to publish in a similar neat style a selection of plates of some of those magnificent and beautiful old English gardens which, during the reigns of Elizabeth, James I. and II., Charles I. and II., William, Anne, George I. and II., and the early part of that of George III., adorned, embellished, and enriched the mansions of many of our nobility and gentry.

That distinguished writer on the Picturesque, Sir

Uvedale Price, even he regrets with exquisite feeling the destruction of many of our gardens in the old style, arguing for the preservation of the few remains that then existed of their ancient magnificence. Horace Walpole, too, brings to our pleased recollection the ancient style of some of our gardens, when his enthusiasm paints with such delight that art which, to use his own words, 'softens Nature's harshness and copies her graceful touch.' To such, therefore, who wish to view what *engravings* have been given of some of our ancient gardens, I beg to offer the following most scanty and scattered gleanings for their inspection:—

In the *Gardener's Labyrinth*, 'are set forth divers knots and mazes, cunningly handled for the beautifying of gardens;' and two or three of these woodcuts might be copied.*

In the title-page to Gerard's own edition of his *Herball* is a very neat plate of a garden, probably his own 'fine garden' in Holborn, so eulogised by Dr. Bullen and others.

Chauncey's *Herts* exhibits Aspeden Hall with its garden. Respect for the memory of John Lightfoot, the most eminent in Rabbinical learning this country

---

* In the Catalogue of the Harleian MSS., No. 5308, is the following entry :—'Variety of plans for garden plots, wildernesses, &c., neatly drawn on paper, but without any writing at all.'

ever produced, and whose residence at Catherine Hall, Cambridge, causes that spot to be still gazed on with respectful awe, induces one to wish this view of Aspeden (the frequent scene of his happy social visits) was re-engraved. One may say of Lightfoot what was said of Young—'full of benevolence, goodness, and piety.' A beautiful edition of Chauncey has lately come out in two volumes, 8vo., and which exhibits three or four other gardens.

Worlidge, in his *Systema Horticulturæ*, 8vo., 1688, has two engravings by Van Houe, being the form of gardens 'according to the newest models.' Though these may be called very simple models, yet one almost wishes to preserve them out of respect to the author, so frequently does he break forth in praise of gardens.

Kennet's *Parochial Antiquities* gives a good plate of Saresden House and garden, and one or two other gardens.

Dugdale's *Warwickshire* has five or six gardens.

The frontispiece to the seventh edition of London and Wise's *Compleat Gard'ner*, and the two neat cuts of gardens, at page 22; also, in their *Retired Gardener* are several plates of parterres, knots, labyrinths, grass plots and arches, and a plan of Marshal Tallard's garden at Nottingham.

In Bray's *Memoirs of John Evelyn* is a slight etching of the garden at Wootton.

Several plates are worth inspecting in Switzer's *Fruit Gardener*, in his *Ichnographia*, and in his *Hydraulicks*.

Thomas Bowles engraved trellis-work for the entrances into arbors, shady walks, &c.

Langley's *Principles of Gardening*, and James' *Theory and Practice of Gardening* may be seen.

There is rather a curious frontispiece to the *Young Gardner's Director*, by H. Stevenson, 1716, 8vo.; another also in the *Country Gentleman's Vade Mecum*, by Giles Jacob, 1717, 8vo.; and another very neat one as a frontispiece to Charles Evelyn's *Lady's Recreation*.

Buck has given us the curious garden at Honnington Hall, Warwickshire.

The frontispiece to Seely's *Stowe*.

Highmore drew, and Tinney engraved, a set of beautiful views of Hampton Court, Middlesex, *and the gardens*.

The frontispiece to Miller's *Dictionary*, 2 vols., folio, 1731.

The frontispiece to Nourse's *Compania Fœlix*, 8vo.

Lawrence's *Clergyman's Recreation* gives two plates. One of these, I presume, exhibits his own garden and vicarage house; if so, this should be an additional motive for our preserving this little testimony to his memory. He is well deserving of it from the zeal with which he throughout mentions the pleasures of a garden.

Many of the old gardens at Oxford may be seen in the curious views given of them in Loggan's *Oxonia Illustrata*; in the very neat ones in Skelton's *Oxonia Restaurata* and in Williams' *Oxonia Depicta*. Beeverell, in his *Delices de la Grande Bretagne*, has given reduced copies of some of them, and also of the Cambridge gardens. Loggan has also given some of the latter ones in his *Cantabrigia Illustrata*.*

* James Dallaway, in his interesting *Anecdotes of the Arts*, pays the following tribute to Oxford :—' Oxford is not more distinguished for beauty as a city, than for the number and pleasantness of its gardens and public resorts. The "cathedral length of trees" at Christ Church, the bowers of Merton, the happy effects of modern gardening at St. John's, and of the style *of the last age* in Trinity and New Colleges, with the delightful retreats on the banks of the Cherwell, at Magdalene, compose environs of infinite amenity. The English Academus enjoys its "studious walks and shades" which yield to those of Athens only on account of the revolutions of our climate.'

It is scarcely possible to think on Oxford without the mind recurring to the recollection of the late Dr. Thomas Warton. No man took greater pleasure than he did in conversing, not only on its ancient college gardens, but on those that in his youth existed in the adjacent counties. His poems exhibit the richest imagery when painting the scenes of Nature. Flattery cannot now 'sooth the dull cold ear of death,' and therefore let me devote a very brief tribute to that mild and good man, by quoting a few lines from one who knew him well : ' Before I enter on the subject of his great literary abilities I must mention what is much more estimable, the virtu and goodness of his heart. Truth, honour, and a generosity of disposition, endeared him to all who knew him. From an unsuspecting

There is a cut of a little garden in the title-page to Burton's *Leicestershire*.

Morant's *Essex* has a plan of Colchester, which gives the gardens belonging to a great many of their private houses. This reminds one of what the *Encyclopædia of Gardening*, at page 1070, says: 'Formerly the tradesmen of Chelmsford and Colchester were much attached to the culture of florists'

honesty of heart flowed a gentleness, a simplicity of manners, which rendered him highly endearing to his friends. He was above all the little evasions of cold and selfish hearts; a benevolence extensive gave a lustre to every virtue. He never did a *mean* action: always exalted, always excellent, noble, and elevated in his sentiments, his character was unsullied. He was eminent for all the mild and social virtues. The goodness and sweetness of his disposition were remarkable. Such was the elevation of his mind, that he appeared totally above taking notice of what so often discomposes even men of sense and learning. One of the chief parts in his character was benevolence. How great must be the charitable temper he possessed when his income, which solely arose from his merit and literary labours, was great part of it spent in benevolent actions! As he was the least ostentatious of men, much of his generous goodness was concealed, yet much was known to the world; the rest to only his Creator, to good angels, and to himself; his beneficence, like himself, was silent and sincere.'

Let me apply to him what Swift's Lord Cork says of Archbishop Herring: 'Honour and reverence will attend his name while this world lasts; happiness and glory will remain with him for ever.'

I cannot also prevent myself from appealing to my reader in the concluding words of Boileau's epitaph on Racine: 'O toi qui que tu sois, qui la piété attire en ce saint lieu, plains dans un si excellent homme la triste destinée de tous les mortels; et quelque grande idée que puisse te donner de lui sa réputation, souviens-toi que ce sont des prières, et non pas de vains éloges qu'il te demande.'

flowers, and they still continue to be so in a considerable degree.'

Kip has engraved, in folio, from the designs of Knyff, very interesting views of the magnificence of our old gardens, under the title of *Britannia Illustrata*.

Atkyns' *Gloucestershire* gives us many of Kip's views.

Beeverell's *Delices de la Grande Bretagne et de l'Irlande*, 8vo. 12mo., Leide, 1727, gives many views of old English gardens, most of them reduced views from Kip.

Peter Vander, at Amsterdam, published in an oblong 8vo. reduced views from Kip, entitled *Vues des Villes*, in several parts or tomes.

Badeslade published *Thirty-six views of Seats in Kent*, with their gardens; no date, folio; some of them engraved by Kip.

To sum up all, let me again refer to the most beautiful plates ever given of old English gardens, namely, to that at Oxnead Hall, in the second volume of Britton's *Architectural Antiquities*, and to his exquisite copy of Kip's views of the garden at Longleat, in the same splendid volume.

Whether any of the following plates may be worth copying, I leave to others to judge of:—

Isaac de Caux published *Twenty-six plates of Wilton Gardens*. Woollett engraved views of the gardens at Whitton, those at Wilton, and Sir F. Dashwood's at West Wycombe. Vivares also engraved some.

Rysbrake, and also Donowell, gave *Views of Chiswick Gardens;* Chatelain gave those at Stowe; all published by Wilkinson, Bowles, and Laurie. The finest *Views of the Gardens at Stowe* were drawn by Rigaud, and published by *Sarah Bridgeman* in 1739.

Wale drew, and Muller engraved, *A general Prospect of the Gardens at Vauxhall.*

Ant. Walker drew a curious view of Prior Park.

Stainborough House and garden, in Yorkshire, was published by Wilkinson; he also published views of Hampton Court, Middlesex, and its gardens.

Some of the following works may possibly lead to the discovery of *prints* of some of our old gardens, or at least, may contain *descriptions* of some of them:—

Leland's *Itinerary*, some of whose pages I should think must offer a few choice bits of brief gleanings. The *Encyclopædia of Gardening*, at page 69, refers to some of the gardens that Leland mentions.*

Aubrey's *Surrey*, and, no doubt, some of our other county histories.

---

* Leland thus speaks of Guy's Cliff: 'It is a place fit for the Muses; there is sylence; a praty wood; *antra in vivo saxo* (grottoes in the living rock); the river rolling over the stones with a praty noise.'

Lysons' Magna Britannia, Stukeley's *Itinerarium Curiosum*, Lysons' *Environs*, Gough's *British Topography*. That richly interesting work of *Brayley and Britton's*, the *Beauties of England and Wales*, in twenty-six volumes.

Vertue's *Oxford Almanacks* give a few of the old gardens.

Whether Ralph Aggas' bird's-eye view of Oxford delineates any of its gardens, I know not.

Vertue's *Description of Hollar's works*. Hollar engraved Boscobel *with its Garden;* and this *Description* will show his other English views. I faintly recollect one of his plates, being that of a yew-tree, or box-tree, in some garden, with a bower in it. He engraved also Albury, in Surrey, the seat of Lord Arundel, *with its vineyard*.

Did Michael Burgher, the delineator of Plot's *Ancient Mansions*, give us any other English ones? or Van Houe, who engraved the two gardens in Worlidge's *Systema Horticulturæ*, and also the rural frontispiece to his *Systema Agriculturæ?* or Vander Gutch, who engraved for Switzer?

One sees sometimes *Portraits in oil* having *English gardens in the background*, as in the original picture of Sir Philip Sydney, by Zucchero, from which Vertue engraved his very fine print. In the Ashmolean Museum is, among others of the family, a portrait of

Tradescant, the son, *in his garden*, with a spade in his hand. In a *Catalogue of pictures*, sold by Southgate in 1826, was 'a small whole-length portrait of Queen Henrietta Maria *in a garden*, with her two favourite spaniels, by Honthorst.' In a *Catalogue of authentic portraits in oil*, sold by Horatio Rodd, in 1824, is a whole-length of William Stukeley *in his curious garden*. In some of Netcher's pictures one often sees gardens, orange groves, and statues. So also in many of Mompert's.

CHAPTER II.

DESCRIPTION OF MANY GARDENS IN ENGLAND AND SCOTLAND, IN 1714.

WHETHER it is likely to obtain prints or drawings of any of our ancient gardens, described or alluded to in any of the following works, I know not:—

The first is from the *Spectator*, which originally came out in small folio weekly numbers, a part of each number being appropriated to advertisements In that of August 14th, 1711, appears:—'At Westerham, in Kent, within twenty miles of London, a dwelling-house is to be sold, with stables, coach-house, brew-house, and complete conveniences of all kinds, together with *a very fine garden laid out in terraces*, and planted with variety of greens and fruit trees. Enquire at the Lady Reeve's, at Westerham, or at Mr. Wilkinson's Chambers, in Searle's Court, in Lincoln's Inn, London.'

Peck, in his *Desiderata Curiosa*, quotes the following description of Theobald's, from a MS. *Life of Lord Burleigh*:—'He greatlie delighted in making gardens, fountains, walks, which at Theobald's were perfected most costly, beauteyfully, and pleasantly, where one might walk twoe myle in the walks before he came to the end.'

The *Topographer*, Vol. II., after giving an interesting description of Ashridge Abbey, says, 'The house is entirely surrounded by walks, within which is *the old garden*, much neglected and growing wild. Here are large laurels and yew-trees grown to an unusual size!' Is there, among the archives of the Bridgewater family, no view of the garden belonging to this once most venerable and most curious of all curious spots?

The *Magna Britannia* speaks thus of Deepdene, near Dorking: 'The house, gardens, orchards, and boscages are placed in a most pleasant and delightful solitude. In the garden, which may seem a second Eden, there are twenty-one sorts of thyme, many rare flowers, and choice plants. On the south side of the hill is a vineyard of many acres, and on the west a laboratory and neat oratory. Where under heaven can be a sweeter place?'

Sir H. Wotton calls the garden at Ware Park 'a delicate and diligent curiosity, without parallel among foreign nations.'

Stebbing Shaw, in his *Tour to the West*, after describing Holm-Lacy, thus mentions the beauty and magnificence of its gardens: 'The gardens to the south front are all in King William's style of fortifications, surrounded with yew-hedges, cut in variety of forms, according to the taste of that time. Some, indeed, have been suffered to outgrow their original shape, and are really beautiful. As there are so few relics of these sorts of antiquities now remaining, 'tis pity not to have the power of such an inspection sometimes; this is certainly a very fit object for that purpose, and will, in all probability, long continue so.'*

* These once celebrated gardens were the delight of that Viscount Scudamore, whose zeal was almost the occasion of throwing the whole county of Hereford 'into one entire orchard;' and who produced an apple

'. . . . whose pulpous fruit,
With gold irradiate, and vermilion, shone tempting.'

To view these gardens, Laud frequently visited Holm-Lacy, and they were a great solace to Lord Scudamore, when his friend, Buckingham, was stabbed by Felton. Lord Scudamore stood next to the Duke when that blow was struck, and the grief which that event caused induced him to retire from public life to Holm-Lacy. He closed a life of honour in 1671. I believe it was this Lord Scudamore who introduced Milton, when in his bloom of life, to the aged Galileo, in Tuscany, after he had been twice in the Inquisition. I gather this from the *Mornings in Spring*, where Nathan Drake has given an interesting account of that meeting.

The dagger with which Felton stabbed Buckingham was *barbed* at the end like an arrow, so that when once it was stricken home into the flesh, it must almost certainly be fatal. The dagger is preserved at Newnham Paddox, in Leicestershire, the seat of the Earl of Denbigh, whose possession of it seems to arise from his ancestor, the first earl, having been married to Buckingham's sister.

At Richmond Green, in the gardens of Sir M. Decker, 'is said to be the longest and highest hedge of holly that was ever seen, with several other hedges of evergreens, vistas cut through woods, grottos, fountains, a canal, a decoy, summer-house, and hot-houses, in which the Indian fruit, called Ananas, was first brought to maturity.'

Are there any views of Sir Hugh Platt's garden in St. Martin's Lane, or of Lord Bacon's at Gorhambury? Whoever reads his chapter 'Of Gardens,' will join me in regretting that we have no vestige remaining of that garden which his great mind formed for the purpose of showing what *the true pleasure of a garden* consists of. In the second volume of Malone's publication of *Aubrey's Letters* are preserved a few fragments of Gorhambury.

It would be curious and pleasant if one could obtain drawings or engravings of any of the following gardens:

Dr. Turner's, at Wells, whom Gerard calls 'that excellent, painefull, and diligent physition;' and of whom Dr. Pulteney, in reference to his *Herball*, says, 'He will appear to have exhibited uncommon diligence and great erudition, and fully to deserve the character of an original writer.'

The Duke of Somerset's at Sion House.

The old garden at Hatfield, 'a labyrinth of clipt yew hedges.'

Sir Edmund Anderson's at Harefield, who had 'a faire house, standing on the edge of the hill, the River Colne passing near the same thro' the pleasant meadows and sweet pastures, yielding both delight and profit.'

Dr. Pulteney tells us that Lyle, in his *Herbal*, speaks of 'the pleasant garden of *James Champaigne*, the deer friende and lover of plantes.'

The gardens at Audley End, the erection of which mansion cost 190,000*l*.

Those of John de Franqueville, a London merchant, and of Hugh Morgan, apothecary to Queen Elizabeth.

Loader's, in Greenwich, who Evelyn says 'grew so rich as to build a house in the street, with gardens, orangeries, canals, and other magnificence.'

Evelyn's pleasant villa at Deptford, which had 'a fine garden for walks, trees, and a little green-house.'

That at Ham House, Middlesex, where (says Evelyn) 'the parterres, flower gardens, orangeries, groves, avenues, courts, statues, perspectives, fountains, aviaries, and all this at the banks of the sweetest river in the world, must needs be admirable.'

The gardens at Beddington, the celebrated seat of the Carews.

Those 'pleasant walks and topiary works,' that Plot so warmly speaks of as adorning Brewood, and other seats in Staffordshire.

The gardens at Cannons, on some of the musical days at which place, such was the eagerness to hear Handel (and, no doubt, to view the garden), that fifty Hackney coaches, crammed with company, have been counted in one day at Edgeware.

That of Lady Brooke's at Hackney, 'one of the neatest and most celebrated in England.'

That garden at Edger, which (as Switzer informs us) was the very last Mr. London superintended, belonging to the Earl of Carnarvon, one of the most illustrious and most noble-spirited geniuses of this age, who, notwithstanding his familiarity in all other arts and sciences, seems to have made gardening and the august embellishments of his country seat, his darling and favourite employ.*

---

* Switzer thus goes on: 'And shall we not at least just mention the Right Honourable the Earls of Scarbrough, Sunderland, Rochester, and Chesterfield; the Dukes of Montague, Bolton, and Kent; not to omit, and that for many weighty reasons, the late, and no less eminent in his love to gardening and agriculture, the present illustrious and most noble Duke of Devonshire, with many others amongst some of the greatest ornaments of arts and sciences, especially gardening, that history has produced, in their several *chateaux* and *seats* of *Stanstead, Althorp, New Park, &c*, in those of *Boughton, Hawkwood,* and *Wrest,* and last of all, in that stupendous performance of Chatsworth.'

Let me add to these the name of Charles Montagu, Earl of Halifax, the warm friend of Addison, whom Tickell alludes to in his elegy on Addison, and which Dr. Drake, in his generous and masterly biographical sketch of Addison, observes, 'may be

The garden at Moor Park, laid out by the Countess of Bedford, celebrated by Dr. Donne, and which Sir W. Temple declared was 'the sweetest place I think that I have seen in my life, at home or abroad: and the remembrance of what it was, is too pleasant ever to forget.'*

Those magnificent gardens at Boughton, in Northamptonshire, which consisted of ninety acres, 'with aviaries, statues, urns, terraces, wildernesses, and curious fountains.'

That of Lady Orford's in Dorsetshire, or that at Stanstead, both alluded to by Horace Walpole.

That which Pope thus describes in a letter to Martha Blount, on his road to Bath: 'I lay one night termed, without dispute, one of the most affecting elegies in our language ':—

'While speechless o'er thy closing grave we bend,
Accept these tears, thou dear departed friend!
Oh, gone for ever! take this long adieu,
And sleep in peace with thy own Montagu.'

* R. O. Cambridge, in No. 118 of the *World*, written in 1755, says, 'Sir W. Temple, in his *Gardens of Epicurus*, expatiates with great pleasure on that at Moor Park, in Hertfordshire; yet after he has extolled it as the pattern of a perfect garden, for use, beauty, and magnificence, he rises to nobler images, and in a kind of prophetic spirit points out a higher style, free and unconfined. The prediction is verified upon the spot; and it seems to have been the peculiar destiny of that delightful place to have passed through all the transformations and modes of taste, having exercised the genius of the most eminent artists successively, and serving as a model of perfection in each kind.'

at Rousham, which is the prettiest place for waterfalls, jetts, ponds, inclosed with beautiful scenes of green and hanging wood, that ever I saw.'

The ancient garden at Denton Court, in Kent, with its high clipped hedges, terraces, and mount, and near which winds for a mile or two a most beautiful green valley that affords the most pleasing sequestered walk, and where the poet Gray (I am quoting from that most pleasing compilation, the *Topographer*) used to delight in many of its recluse scenes.

Mr. Braithwaite's gardens at Durham, in Gloucestershire, the description of which rural garden takes up no less than fourteen of Switzer's pages, 'notwithstanding the happy possessor bears no higher character than that of a private gentleman. I never in my whole life saw so agreeable a place for the sublimest studies as this is.'

The gardens of Lord William Russell (beheaded in 1683) at Stratton, near Winchester, 'one of the best of masters, as well as gardeners;' and whose severe fate Switzer most gratefully laments.*

* The Rev. John Lawrence, in his *Clergyman's Recreation*, thus mentions another garden near Winchester: 'I have myself seen the summer Bon Cretien in the garden of my worthy friend, Dr. Wickart, now Dean of Winchester, bear plenty of noble, large fruit, betwixt twenty and thirty feet high. There also I have eaten excellent figs from a prosperous tree, even the same that afforded some to King James I., near a hundred years ago, as appears (I think) from a memorandum on the wall.'

A garden at Hillingdon, near Uxbridge, must have been a noted one, belonging to a 'most curious and learned gentleman in the art of gardening, Samuel Richardson, Esq.,' whom Bradley so frequently mentions in his *New Improvements;* and in the churchyard of which village he mentions the noted *Yew-trees* there, after saying that the leaves of the *Yew* are so small that it is possible to bring them to any form we desire, as men, beasts, birds, ships, and the like, and in which churchyard (by-the-bye) poor Dr. Dodd (whose fate once made so much noise) and his wife are both buried, and '*after life's fretful fever, sleep well.*'*

Bradley, in the above volume, notices no less than

* 'To give new beauties to your garden,' says the Rev. J. Lawrence, in his *Clergyman's Recreation,* 'none in my mind is to be compared to the yew, which is so tonsile, and grows so very thick and beautiful with clipping, and withal bids defiance to the hardest winters, that it is the best and most lasting ornament in a garden. To make one in love with these hedges, you need only take a walk in the Physic Gardens at Oxford, where you are presented with all that art and nature can do, to make the things most agreeable to the eye.'

Cobbett, when relating many particulars of the Yew in his *Woodlands* (for his pen has an original power in describing these subjects, he himself telling us, that his 'heart and mind is wrapped up in everything belonging to the gardens, the fields, and the woods'), observes that 'It resists all weather, stands uninjured on the bleakest hills, where even the scrubbiest of thorns and underwood will hardly live. Big as the head of this tree generally is, in proportion to its trunk, most heavily laden as it constantly is with leaf, forming as it does such a hold for the wind, neither head nor trunk ever flinches, though in situations where it would be impossible thirteen times Mr. Fairchild's garden at Hoxton; and frequently speaks of the delight of a Mr. Balle's garden at Campden House.

The curious garden of the vicarage house at St. Just, near Falmouth, is, I am told, now kept up in nearly its ancient style; so, I am told, is Lord Falmouth's garden at Flushing, near Penryn.

It is too late in the day now to expect to obtain drawings of any of those gardens, 'large, beautiful, and planted with trees,' which the citizens of London

to make an oak grow, and where no other large tree could be prevented from being blown out of the ground.' In his description of the *Crab* he says, 'In hedges it is very beautiful in the spring, and also in independent trees, covered with blossoms as bright as those of the carnation, and a great deal larger. When the coppices are cut, the crabs, if they go up in a single stem, are generally left as the oaks are; and in the month of May, the garlands presented by the crab-trees, while the primroses bespangle the ground beneath, and while the birds are singing all around, certainly gives up altogether something more delightful than almost anything else accessible to our senses.' In his *English Gardener*, he thus mentions an almost unheeded shrub, 'The *Box* is at once the most efficient of all possible things, and the prettiest plant that can possibly be conceived: the colour of its leaf, the form of its leaf, its docility as to height, width, and shape, the compactness of its little branches, its great durability as a plant, its thriving in all sorts of soils and in all sorts of aspects, its freshness under the hottest sun, and its defiance of all shade and all drip; these are beauties and qualities which, for ages upon ages, have marked it out as the chosen plant for this very important purpose.' And after describing how it should be clipped, he says, 'If there is a more neat and beautiful thing than this in the world, all I can say is, that I never saw that thing.'

had in the time of Henry II., and which Fitzstephen mentions; or of that 'garden faire' at Windsor, in Henry the Fifth's reign, where the thick

> '.... bewis, and the leaves greene,
> Beschudit all the alleyes that there were;'

which the *Encyclopædia of Gardening* tells us James I. of Scotland describes, when a prisoner there; or even of the 'exceeding fair gardens within the mote, and the orchardes without,' at Wresehill Castle, which Leland mentions; or of that vineyard and garden in Holborn which, in the reign of Henry III., was given to the conventical Church of Ely; or of the three gardens and dove-house belonging to the once richly decorated Church of St. Helen's, Bishopsgate Street; or of that garden (perhaps near the one which Gerard afterwards rendered so famous) in Holborn, containing, with its orchard, about forty acres (on the site of which the present Hatton Garden is built), the strawberries in which were so excellent, that even *Richard* (Garrick's Richard) beseeched my Lord of Ely to 'send for some of them.'

Shakespeare reminds us of another garden: for Dallaway, in his *Supplementary Anecdotes of Gardening* annexed to his invaluable edition of Walpole's *Anecdotes*, remarks, that the poet thus mentions a garden of those times, in the first Act of *Love's Labour Lost*:—

> 'Thy curious knotted garden.'

We have innumerable instances of the great poet's attachment to *Botany*. Whoever painted the violet, the crimson drops 'i' th' bottom of a cow-slip,' and the 'winking' mary-buds, with a sweeter pencil than his? The same may be said as to his distribution of the flowers by the pretty Perditta, by Ophelia, those in *Cymbeline*, and by Friar Laurence. We have many of his remarks on general *Horticulture*. One may describe modern or landscape gardening by applying to it those lines of his, when he is speaking of an art which he says '*shares with great creating nature :*' viz., the art of grafting the apple on the crab; for he calls it

'. . . . an art
Which does mend nature, change it rather ; but
The art itself is nature.'

If my reader smiles at what he may call this trifling, reminding him of 'another garden,' let me shelter myself under the unerring authority of Thomas Warton, who, in his *History of English Poetry*, declares that 'every hovel to which Shakespeare alludes interests curiosity.'

W. Withers, in his letter to Sir W. Scott, gives the following quotation from the late Nathaniel Kent, and I here insert that quotation merely because Mr. Kent has thus reminded us that Shakespeare was aware of the danger of improper *pruning:*

'I shall close my observations on this interesting subject with a word of advice, by way of guarding against a pernicious practice which, though hitherto unknown in this county, has lately got some footing in it—I mean the *infamous* custom which prevails in some counties of pruning up trees, divesting them of their corner or lateral branches. When a plant is very young, it is sometimes allowable to a certain distance, but should always be done with great caution; but when trees have begun to form themselves it is a sort of *murder*. It stops the growth and produces extreme deformity; for the sap in the spring of the year being checked in its natural diffusion into the number of branches into which it used to flow becomes distorted

> "*As knots, by the conflux of meeting sap,
> Infect the sound pine, and divert his grain,
> Tortive and errant, from his course of growth.*"'

In a large view of London, as it appeared in 1563 (and of which there is a reduced copy in Pennant's *London*, and a neat copy thereof is also sold by Harris, at the corner of St. Paul's), there is a garden adjoining the bull-baiting ground, nearly opposite Queenhithe; it also exhibits the Strand Gardens, Privy Gardens, and that of the Convent, or Covent, Garden.

I am indebted to the rich pages of the *Encyclo-*

pædia of Gardening for the whole of the following notices of our ancient gardens :—

In Part I., Chapter IV., it mentions, amongst a great many celebrated old gardens, Dr. Sherard's at Eltham, 'one of the richest gardens England ever possessed,' immortalised, says Pulteney, by the pen of Dillenius; and Collinson's 'fine garden' at Mill Hill. And in the subsequent pages (amongst an infinite variety) I select only the following :—

Gabions, near North Mimms.

In Henry the Seventh's time, the seat of the father of the illustrious Sir Thomas More. The gardens were then, and in the succeeding reign, celebrated for their splendour in the ancient taste.

Theobald's Park.

The gardens were large, and ornamented with labyrinths, canals, and fountains. There were nine knots artificially and exquisitely made, one of them in imitation of the king's arms.

Blenheim.

The flower garden was an oval, with a basin of water in the centre, and radiating walks, after the plan of that of Madame de Pompadour, at Versailles.

Unhappily (as we think) it has lately been destroyed, and an aviary erected on its site.

Heythrop.

The grounds chiefly in the ancient taste, with curious artificial cascades.

Troy House, near Monmouth.

This seat was famed for its gardens in Charles the First's time, and especially for its delicious fruits. The same gardens were famous in Henry the Eighth's time.

Ingestree Hall.

A respectable Elizabethan edifice, surrounded by grounds in the ancient style, but in a great degree modernized by the present possessor.

Bretby Park.

A fine old structure, taken down some years ago, said to have been surrounded with gardens disposed after the plan of Versailles, with terraces, statues, and fountains.*

* See a *Bird's-eye View*, by Kip, and the *Topographer*, Vol. II.

Haddon Hall.

The terrace gardens remain, and consist of terraces ranged one above the other, each having a stone balustrade.

Alton Grove, near Nottingham.

The gardens on the side of a hill, originally in the ancient taste, but lately remodelled.

Thoresby Park.

The gardens were in part constructed in the French style, by the late Duchess of Kingston.

Exton Hall, near Stratton.

A grand Elizabethan edifice, with a park of one thousand five hundred and ten acres, planted in the ancient style, by London and Wise; the gardens have long been famous, and the water and cascades much admired.

Lake House, near Amesbury.

A truly picturesque edifice, with bay windows, gables, yew-hedges, terraces, &c., in the genuine style of the last age.

Oxton House, Devon.

The grounds, which had been laid out at great expense, in the old style, are modernized.

Leeswood, near Mold.

The grounds occupy a fine slope, and were laid out by Switzer above a century ago; the magnificent iron gateway still remains.

Pentre, Pembroke.

The house is in a pleasant rural spot, embosomed in trees; the gardens in the old style, carefully kept up; the whole greatly admired.

Powis Castle.

The ascent by two immense terraces, rising one above the other, connected by steps, and ornamented by vases, statues, and other antique remains. There were hanging gardens in imitation of those of St. Germains, composed of a series of terraces, connected by flights of steps cut out of the solid rock, with water-works, &c.*

* See Sir Uvedale Price's remarks on Powis Castle, in his 'sharp but most candid and gentleman-like letter to Mr. Repton. The spirit of these pages (87 and 88), with other rich ones, in his writings on landscape gardening, lend (to borrow a quotation of his own)

'. . . . a fire
E'en to the dullest peasant.'

Hatton House, near Calder.

A venerable ancient house; the grounds, till lately, exhibited one of the most perfect specimens of the old style in the county, or perhaps in Scotland, with artificial cascades, fountains, alcoves, terraces, &c.

Woodhouselee, near Roslin.

A venerable and romantic house and grounds; the latter remarkable for containing the largest silver fir-tree in the county, a fine terrace, walk, and superb holly-hedge. Some curious ornaments, in the geometric style of gardening, were obliterated when the grounds were re-modelled in 1787.

Castle Glamis.

A very ancient building; the grounds in the ancient style.

Crathes, near Aberdeen.

An excellent kitchen garden, in the old style, with magnificent holly-hedges, abundance of prolific fruit-trees, and venerable exotic shrubs.

The following account of some English and Scotch gardens is given in *A Journey through England and Scotland*, by Daniel Defoe, written in 1714, 3 vols. 8vo.

Cheveley.

The seat of the late Lord Dover, which, for its situation, gardens, and parks, vies with anything we have seen abroad.

Euston Hall.

The seat of the Duke of Grafton, and built by the late Lord Arlington, is a palace worthy of his quality, with a parterre as fine as ever I saw.

New Hall, near Witham.

Built by Henry VIII., and called for its charming situation *Beau-lieu,* is still worth seeing; the avenue of trees from the great road is majestic, being nearly an English mile long, very broad, and the trees large and regular.

Wanstead.

The noble seat of Sir Richard Child, with the finest gardens in the world. You descend from the salon into the parterre, which hath a canal in the middle; on the right a wilderness, and on the left a fine green walk, which ends in a banqueting-house. On one side of this green walk stands the green-house, finely adorned with statues, and uncommonly furnished with greens: while behind this green-house are variety of high-hedged walks, affording delicious vistas. At the bottom of the canal is a bowling-green encircled with grottos and seats, with antique statues between each seat; this bowling-green is separated by a balustrade of iron from another long green walk, which leads you to another long canal.

Cranburne Lodge.

Built by the late Earl of Ranelagh, on the top of a hill, in Windsor Forest; the gardens are very large and very elegant.

The Earl of Cardigan's, near Reading.

When his avenues, gravel walks, gardens, and other plantations are finished, it will be one of the most agreeable seats in England.

Ashridge.

Saw the fine seat of *Ashridge,* belonging to the Duke of Bridgewater. The family of the Drakes have also a very fine seat nigh this, with very fine gardens. Uborn, belonging to the Duke of Wharton, with its gardens, &c., is inferior to very few in the kingdom. He hath also in this county another seat which he more delights in, called *Winchenden,* which is very noble; the gardens and orangery are not inferior to many in the kingdom.

Gerrard's Cross.

The charming seat of the Duke of Portland; the house, the gardens, and the wood are disposed with as great magnificence as can be imagined; nothing can be finer than the terraces by which to descend from the apartments to the gardens.

Hampton Court.

The front to the east, all of free-stone, is very noble, looking into the park over a noble parterre a good half-mile long, embellished with vases, statues, gravel and green walks, and separated from the park by a balustrade of iron. On the north side there is also a little garden, walled in, with a most curious labyrinth; while from the palace along the river side is a noble terrace walk which leads to the bowling-green, where in each corner is a large pavilion.

Richmond.

The Earl of Rochester's gardens, ascending the hill in an artfully confused manner, are very curious and wonderful.

Lord Carleton hath a pretty little seat betwixt Petersham and Ham, with fine gardens; and Mr. Serjeant Darnell hath also a very magnificent palace, lately built, at Petersham, with gardens.

On Richmond Green is a fine house and gardens, made by Sir Charles Hedges, but now belonging to Sir Matthew Decker, which are very curious. The longest, largest, and highest hedge of holly I ever saw is in this garden, with several other hedges of evergreens, vistas cut through woods, grottos with fountains, and a fine canal running up from the river. His duckery, which is an oval pond bricked round, and his pretty summer-house by it in which to drink a bottle, his stove-houses, which are always kept of an equal heat for his citrons and other Indian plants, with gardeners brought from foreign countries to manage them, are very curious and entertaining. Mr. Heydegger, director of the king's balls, hath also a very handsome house and gardens on this Green; as hath also Colonel Dunkam, of the Guards, with a large dancing-room adjoining. To the eastward of this Green, Justice Byers hath a most noble seat and gardens. To particularise every little villa here would make my letter a volume. I will only add that the Scotch Marquis of Lothian hath a fine seat at Mashgate, half a mile from Richmond; and a mile further east Mr. Temple hath built a most noble one at East Sheen, where the famous Sir William Temple made those fine gardens he so often mentions in his writings, and so much delighted in.

Bushey Park.

That charming seat of the late Lord Hallifax, the Mæcenas of England, the great patron of learning and learned men. As he had a good taste in everything, you may believe there is nothing wanting to the embellishment of this place; the cascade is reckoned a masterpiece of its kind, and the whole worth the curiosity of a traveller.

In two hours from Hampton Court you come to Twickenham, a village remarkable for its abundance of curious seats, of which that of Boucher, the famous gamester, would pass in Italy for a delicate palace. The Earl of Mar, the Earl of Strafford, the Earl of Bradford, Lord Brooke, Lord Dunbar, and Lady Falkland, have each their pretty villas in this parish; but I think that of Secretary Johnstoun, for the elegancy and largeness of his gardens, his terrace on the river, and the situation of his house, makes much the brightest figure here: his house may be more properly called a plantation, being in the middle betwixt his parterre, his kitchen garden, his fruit garden, and his pleasure garden and wilderness. The house is exactly after the model of the country seats in Lombardy, being of two galleries, with rooms going off on each side. The gallery on the ground floor makes a hall fronting the pleasure garden, and a parlour fronting the parterre which, when the doors are open, gives you a delicious prospect of the whole; on each side are five rooms more, adorned with a very good collection of pictures; and in the division betwixt the hall and parlour, on each side, is a staircase that leads you up to the gallery above, containing the same number of rooms. His fine octagon, for the entertainment of his friends at the end of his green-house, I think, is too nigh his house, and I think very much spoils the symmetry of it; it would have stood better and seemed more rural either at his grotto at the west end of his parterre in his wilderness, or at his mount at the west end of his pleasure garden. He has as good a collection of fruit of all sorts, as most gentlemen in England. His slopes for his vines, of which he makes some hogsheads a year, are very particular. Dr. Bradley, of the Royal Society, who hath written so much upon gardening, ranks him amongst the first-rate gardeners in England. The Earl of Strafford's house, which lies next to Mr. Johnstoun's, with its offices, are very noble; his gardens also spacious, but not so much to the riverside, are adorned with several gilded statues and vases, which make a very glaring appearance.

A little house, which belonged formerly to Sir Thomas Skipwith, and was improved and inhabited by that great architect, the late Earl of Mar, with its hanging gardens to the river, is well worth the curiosity of a traveller, as is also that of Sir Godfrey Kneller, the famous face-painter, with several others in this large village, which would be too tedious for a letter.

Kew Green.

Mr. Molineux hath a fine seat here with excellent gardens, said to have the best fruit in England, collected by that great statesman and gardener, Lord Capel.

Isleworth.

Moses Hart, the Jew, hath a noble seat and offices in this village, with fine gardens, inferior to few palaces. Mr. Barker's gardens, park, and avenues, cut through his wood to the river, are worth the curiosity of a stranger.

Sutton Court.

That celebrated seat of the late Earl of Falconbridge, and I must own that the house, furniture, pictures, and gardening, are well worth the curiosity of a stranger. It belongs to Sir Thomas Frankland. I saw here a great and curious piece of antiquity, the eldest daughter of Oliver Cromwell, still fresh and gay,

though of a great age. Sir Stephen Fox's house
adjacent is much finer outside, and a regular palace
a-la-moderne, with very extensive gardens; but Sutton
Court is *une bijoux;* it hath three parterres from the
three fronts of the house, each finely adorned with
statues. The gardens are irregular, but that, I think,
adds to their beauty, for every walk affords variety;
the hedges, grottos, statues, mounts, and canals, are so
many surprising beauties. Near Sutton Court, General
Witham hath built a most magnificent seat of free-
stone, and is laying out also spacious gardens.

Canterbury.

Mr. Taybour's gardens at Byfronts are indeed
worth seeing, as also Sir Basil Dixwel's, on the skirts
of Parham Downs, near this city.

Tunbridge Wells.

Within three miles of this place is a venerable
old seat which they told me belonged to the family of
the Villiers, Dukes of Buckingham (but now out of
order), called Sommer-hill. It's pity so beautiful a
place should be so neglected, for its situation is noble,
and its gardens have been very large; I could see
above fifty miles in full view from its apartments.

Lewes

is the most romantic situation I ever saw; it consists of six parishes, in which gentlemen's seats, adjoining one another, with their gardens up hill and down hill, compose the town.

Chichester.

The Earl of Scarbrough's seat, at some miles distance, is *une veritable bijoux;* the large avenue, a view cut through a wood, the stables, the gardens, and every thing else, are nobly disposed.

Carshalton,

where I visited the fine gardens of Sir W. Scawen.

Epsom.

There are several very good seats in and about Epsom. That of Lord Guilford, called Durdans, at the extremity of the village, was built by the Earl of Barclay out of the materials of Nonsuch, a royal palace in this neighbourhood, built by Henry VIII., and given by King Charles II. to the Duchess of Cleveland, who pulled it down and sold the materials. This house of Durdans is built *a-la-moderne* of free-stone; the front to the garden, and that to the Downs, are very noble; the apartments within are also very regular, and in the garden is the most charming grove imaginable; famous for that scene of love between Lord Grey and his lady's sister, which you have read of. Lord Baltimore's gardens are also fine; the house is old, but the chapel is the neatest little thing in the world. Mr. Ward's, on Clay Hill, is a delicious palace. The late Sir James Bateman had also a delicate seat at some miles distance; but what charmed me more than anything hereabouts is the river of Carshalton, which environs Sir William Scawen's garden in a square; it is full of fish, and makes a pretty cascade in going out. Within a mile of Epsom is Aysted, belonging to Mr. Fielding, brother to the Earl of Denbigh, which, for its situation, park, and gardens, is inferior to nothing of its size that I have seen in England.

Wimbledon.

The noble seat of the Duke of Leeds, and in a majestic situation. You have three several beautiful prospects from his garden, and the variety is the more diverting that it is in every walk; you can turn nowhere but your view fixes on something new. Sir Theodore Janssen, the French banker, hath also a very delicious seat in this village, which insensibly leads you to the bowling-green of Putney, whither the citizens resort twice a week, and where I have seen pretty deep play. At Putney are several charming seats with their large gardens, fish-ponds, and groves, and indeed the whole parish is one continued garden. At Parson's Green, saw an old seat of the Earl of Peterborough, with fine gardens.

Cambridge.

Visited that worthy old gentleman, Sir Robert Cotton, at his villa of Hatley St. George, a seat worthy of so great and good a man. He hath a noble collection of original paintings, and his house and gardens everywhere answer the grandeur of the first quality.

When the Stuarts came to the throne the space that then separated London and Westminster was filled with several noble palaces and their delicate gardens along the side of the River Thames, viz.: those of the Earl of Essex, Duke of Norfolk, Somerset House, the Savoy, Worcester House, Exeter House, Bedford House, Salisbury House, York House, Northumberland House, and Whitehall; but now most of these splendid palaces are pulled down, and with their gardens built into spacious streets.

Great Marlborough Street, which though not a square, surpasses anything that is called a street, in the magnificence of its buildings and gardens, and inhabited all by prime quality.

Montague House.

A fine garden and terrace behind; the great collection of original paintings are well worth the curiosity of a stranger, as also the statues in the garden.

Burlington Palace.

Behind is a noble parterre or garden which, in a city, makes it very delicious.

Gray's Inn

hath a very large garden with a noble terrace, from whence you have a full view to Hampstead.

Lincoln's Inn.

Its new square fronting the garden, I think one of the greatest beauties about London; the garden is large, full of fine statues, and the walks well kept.

Bedfordshire

is such another fertile county as Buckinghamshire, strewed everywhere with noblemen and gentlemen's seats. The Duke of Kent, chief of the ancient family of the Gray's, hath a very magnificent noble seat, with large parks, avenues, and fine gardens.

Cashioberry.

Its gardens and park are beautiful and spacious.

Cannons.

The disposition of the avenues, gardens, statues, painting, and the house of Cannons, suits the genius and grandeur of its great master. The chapel, which is already finished, hath a choir of vocal and instrumental music, as the royal chapel; and when his Grace goes to church, he is attended by his Swiss guards, ranged as the Yeoman of the guards; his music also plays when he is at table; he is served by gentlemen in the best order; and I must say that few German sovereign princes live with that magnificence, grandeur, and good order. He is that Mr. Bridges whom you knew Paymaster-General in Flanders, son to the Lord Chandos, an ancient and noble family, of which there have been three Knights of the Garter in several reigns: he was created Earl of Carnarvon by King George, and on his father's decease, Duke of Chandos. As he got a great estate by being Paymaster to all the English armies abroad, no man ever made a better use of it by his generosity, hospitality, and charity; of which there are many instances that would be too long for a letter, and, I think, not to my purpose. You ascend the great avenue to Cannons from the town of Edgware, by a fine iron gate, with the duke's arms and supporters on the stone pillars of the gate, with balustrades of iron on each side, and two neat lodges in the inside; this avenue is near a mile long, and three coaches may go abreast; in the middle or half-way of this avenue is a large round basin of water, not unlike that on the great road through Bushey Park to Hampton Court; this avenue fronts an angle of the house, and thereby showing two fronts at once, makes the house seem at a distance the larger. You turn therefore a little to the left to come to the great court, which leads to the saloon and great staircase; and a little further to the left to another court, which leads to the back stairs, now made use of till the great apartments are finished. The house consists of four fronts, all of free-stone, each about one hundred feet wide. The front from the great stairs is to the east, and hath an avenue directly from it down to the parish church, at above half-a-mile distance: the north front is towards the parterre and great canal; the west towards the gardens; and the south looks through a great area where the offices and stables are, down another large avenue which ends in a mountain. The north front is finely adorned with pilasters and columns of stone; and above every window in each front is an antique head, neatly engraved; on the top of all the fronts are statues as big as the life. The saloon, when finished, is to be supported by marble pillars, and painted by Bellucci, as is the great staircase, which is all of marble; most of the steps are already laid, of a great length, and all of one piece of marble; this staircase leads you into the apartments fronting the parterre and grand canal, and consists of a suite of six noble rooms, well-proportioned, finely plastered, and gilt by Pargotti; and the ceilings painted by Bellucci. From these apartments you go into my lord's dressing-room and library, fronting the gardens, and from thence you descend by another fine pair of stairs (which I cannot call back stairs, all painted by Legarr, and balustraded to the top of the house with iron) unto a court, which opens into the great area to the east; in which is the chapel on your right, the kitchens on your left, and lower on each side the stables are finely built, the bottom of the area inclosed with balustrades of iron. The library is a fine spacious room, curiously adorned with books, and statues in wood of the Stoning of St. Stephen, said to be finest of that kind of engraving in the world. The chapel is incomparably neat and pretty, all finely plastered and gilt by Pargotti, and the ceilings and niches painted by Bellucci; there is a handsome altar-piece, and in an alcove above the altar, a neat organ; fronting the altar, above the gate, is a fine gallery for the duke and duchess, with a door that comes from the apartments above, and a staircase that also descends into the body of the chapel, in case of taking the sacrament or other occasion; in the windows of this chapel are also finely painted some parts of the History of the New Testament. In that court which opens into the area is the dining-room, very spacious, and a nobler sideboard of plate than most sovereign princes have; and at the end of it a room for his music, which performs both vocal and instrumental during the time he is at table; he spares no expense to have the best. The parterre fronting the west is separated from the great avenue, and the great court leading to the great staircase by balustrades of iron, as it is also from the gardens on the other side. There is a large terrace walk, from whence you descend to the parterre; this parterre hath a row of gilded vases on pedestals on each side down to the great canal, and in the middle, fronting the canal, is a gladiator, gilded also; through the whole parterre, abundance of statues as big as the life, are regularly disposed. The canal runs a great way, and indeed one would wonder to see such a vast quantity of water in a country where are neither rivers or springs; but they tell me that the Duke hath his water in pipes from the mountains of Stanmore, about two miles off. The gardens are very large and well disposed; but the greatest pleasure of all is that the divisions of the whole, being only made by balustrades of iron and not by walls, you see the whole at once, be you in what part of the garden or parterre you will. In his large kitchen garden there are bee-hives of glass, very curious; and at the end of each of his chief avenues he hath neat lodgings for eight old serjeants of the army, whom he took out of Chelsea College, who guard the whole, go their rounds at night, call the hours as the watchmen do at London to prevent disorders, and wait upon the Duke to chapel on Sundays. It is incredible the ironwork about this noble palace, more I must say than I ever saw elsewhere; and his gentleman told me they are above a hundred servants in family of one degree or another.

Winchester.

At the hospital, founded by Rufus, the master lives like an abbot, hath a very good apartment, with fine gardens, adorned with a canal, and evergreens.

Salisbury.

The Bishop's palace near it is a good old building, with large gardens.

Sherborn.

Mr. Doddington's will be one of the finest, as well as the largest in England, with gardens, park, and waterworks; for the finishing of which he hath left a very great estate to his nephew, Mr. Bubb.

Oxford.

Trinity College. The forth-court opens into a garden kept in extreme good order, planted with evergreens, and the walls round covered all over with yew; and at the bottom of the garden, fronting the square, is a magnificent iron gate. The Physic Garden, situated by the river Cherwell, is a delicious place; it consists of above five acres of ground, the walls are of a square stone, above fourteen feet high; its gates are fine, one of them, of the Composite order, cost 600*l.*; it contains many thousands of useful plants.

Longleat,

though an old seat is very beautiful and large, and the gardens and avenue being full grown are very beautiful and well kept. It cost the late Lord Weymouth a good revenue in hospitality to such strangers as came from Bath to see it.

Lord Cholmondeley's

is a noble old seat, the gardens not inferior to any in England, and one gravel walk the longest I have seen.

Lord Chetwynd's.

A fine old seat, whose gardens are incomparably fine; the walks hedged in with trees fully fifty feet high and thick set, are very august, and open in fine vistas into the adjacent country.

Sir Clement Fisher's, near Coleshill,

is very beautiful; in the middle of a spacious park, with fine gardens, fish-ponds, and a decoy for ducks; it may, altogether, vie with the best seats in England. Most gentlemen keep their packs of dogs, and the whole county of Stafford is very sociable; they have excellent ale, and provisions for almost nothing.

Althorp

is a fine seat in the middle of a charming park; it is moated, but the moat was drained and turned into a garden so fine, that M. La Quintinie took the plan for some of his works at Versailles.

Stanton-Harold.

Earl Ferrer's seat at Stanton-Harold is a noble seat, as big as a little town, and the gardens adorned with statues, very entertaining.

Bratby.

A seat of the Earl of Chesterfield, hath very fine gardens.

Chatsworth.

The gardens are very delightful, pleasant, and stately, adorned with exquisite waterworks.

Nottingham.

When Marshal Tallard was taken prisoner at the battle of Hocklestet, the Government allowed him this pretty town, with the adjacent country for his prison; in the seven years he stayed here he made very fine gardens to the house he lived in.

Castle Howard.

The apartments, furniture, and gardens answer the great genius of its noble master.

A stranger ought not to leave Yorkshire without seeing Sir Thomas Frankland's seat at Thutteby, near the little town of Thirsk, both for its situation and the fineness of its gardens. The parterre is encircled with columns of yew; the wilderness is very neat; and from the whole there is a delicious prospect.

Terragle.

Three miles from Dumfries I saw Terragle, the paternal seat of the unhappy Maxwell, Earl of Nithsdale, who was taken prisoner at Preston, and made his escape out of the Tower. It consists of a large oval court, in which are very stately apartments and large gardens, suitable to the grandeur of so noble a family.*

Drumlanrig.

The hanging gardens cut out of the rock down to the river-side, with waterworks and grottos, do every way answer the great genius of W., Duke of Queensberry.

Traquair.

This palace, built by the Earl of Traquair, who was Lord High Treasurer and Viceroy of Scotland in the reign of Charles I., a great favourite of Archbishop Laud and promoter of his schemes, is a very large noble pile of building of free-stone, situated in a valley on the banks of the Tweed, in the midst of a

* Some interesting remarks on the old gardens of Scotland, may be seen on page 81 of the *Encyclopædia of Gardening.*

wood, through which are cut fine avenues; the gardens are also very spacious.

Yester.

The capital seat of Hay, Marquis of Tweeddale. The rooms of state that run on each side of the saloon, fronting the garden, are very stately; the parterre and garden behind the house is very spacious and fine, rising up by an easy ascent into the park, as those of Lord Rochester's near Richmond. There is a handsome bason, with a *jet d'eau* in the middle of the parterre, with four good statues, upon pedestals, at each corner; there are abundance of evergreens and green slopes regularly disposed; and to the west of the garden, on an artificial mount, is a pleasant summer-house. There is a pretty rapid stream runs by the house, and by its rustling through the trees as it runs through the park, makes the whole very rural. There is a pretty bowling-green by the riverside.

Seaton.

The palace of Seaton stands in the middle of a large plantation of trees, of at least twelve acres, with a large garden to the south and another to the north. The apartments of state are on the second story, and very spacious; three great rooms, at least forty feet high, which they say were finely furnished ever since Mary, Queen of Scots, on her return from France, kept her court there; also two large galleries that were filled with pictures; but on Lord Winton's forfeiture, all these were sold by the Commissioners of Inquiry, or stolen by the servants. There is now not a whole window on that side of the house.

Winton.

About two miles from Seaton is another palace, called Winton. The gardens, which are very spacious, are very well kept.

Musselburgh.

The parterre behind the palace is very large, and nobly adorned with evergreens, and on each side of it spacious gardens.

Edinburgh.

The palace of the Earl of Penmure, in excellent good order, and very fine gardens. The palace of the Earl of Murray; there is a very large parterre or flower garden behind with four hanging walks or terraces to the bottom, where there is a bowling-green, and a handsome pavilion or pleasure-house.

Hewitt's Hospital.

The gardens are very well kept, consisting of

a flower garden, an orchard, and kitchen garden; the house and gardens contain between nine and ten acres.

Palace of Penmure.

In the middle of a great wood. You go up to the house through an avenue cut through the wood, of half-a-mile in length, and 150 feet broad, which gives you a view of the house at once; and on each side of this avenue is a fine hedge, which reaches the branches of the trees of the wood; at the end of this avenue is a large circular outer court for coaches to turn in, and the inner court is balustraded with iron on each side, which gives you a view of the delicious gardens which go quite round the house, and are very well kept, with a great variety of evergreens and grass plots, covered walks, and labyrinths: from these gardens there are eight or nine vistas cut through the wood, with balustrades of iron at every vista, and all the doors of iron.

Castle Gordon.

Fine gardens, and a very spacious deer park.

Palace of Glamis.

As you approach, it strikes you with awe and

admiration, by the many turrets and gilded balustrades at top; you have a full prospect of the gardens on each side, cut out into grass plots, and adorned with evergreens. In the first floor there are thirty-eight fine rooms. When the Pretender lay here, they made eighty-eight beds within the house, for him and his retinue, besides the inferior servants, who lay in the offices out of doors.

Dunkeld.

The Duke of Athol hath here a very noble seat, with large gardens.

Palace of Falkland.

Here were spacious gardens, with a park; but

'*Nunc seges est ubique Troja fuit.*'

Culross.

One cannot imagine a noble palace; a terrace as long and as broad as that at Windsor, with a pavilion at each end, and below the terrace run hanging gardens for half-a-mile, down to the Frith; the design of these gardens was vast. When Lord Mar was laying out his fine gardens at Alloway, he thanked God that Culross was not his, for the expense of keeping it up would ruin him.

Balgony.

Another seat of the Earl of Leveris, whose gardens and park are very spacious.

Palace of Lesly.

There is a noble parterre to the east, cut out into green slopes, adorned with evergreens, that reacheth to the point where the two rivers meet, and from this parterre is a long terrace walk, and under it five several terraces, to which you descend by stately stairs to another square garden by the river-side, with a waterwork in the middle.

Alloway.

The gardens consist of forty-two acres, and the wood, with vistas cut through it, of 150 acres. On the right of the area is a spacious garden with a fine terrace and bowling-green, adorned with the largest evergreens you can see anywhere. To the south is the parterre, spacious, and finely adorned with statues and vases; and from this parterre to the River Forth runs a fine terrace, or avenue, from whence, and from the parterre, you have thirty-two different vistas, each ending on some remarkable seat or mountain: one of them shews you Stirling Castle at four miles distance; another, the Palace of Elphinstone, on the other side of the river; a third, the Castle of Clacmaning. In the middle of this long terrace is a basin of water like that of the Duke of Chandos, at Cannons, in the middle of which is the statue of Cain slaying Abel, and at the end of the river are a pair of pyramidical gates. The avenue to the east, through the wood, is prodigiously long and large, and between each vista, from the parterre, are wildernesses of trees for birds, and little grottos.

Hopton.

The parterre fronting the saloon is longer than that at Cannons, and like it, hath a large bason of water at bottom; it is also adorned with a multitude of statues, on pedestals, as at Cannons; but the views here are prodigiously more extensive. From the terrace to the north of this parterre is the finest view I ever saw anywhere. There are also several vistas from each of the many walks that run from this parterre. This fine palace and garden lies in the middle of a spacious park, well stocked with deer, and environed with a stone wall.

Palace of Hamilton.

A noble parterre adorned with statues, and lower, spacious bounds for a canal and fish-ponds, with large gardens on each side, and at the bottom a fine park. Joining to the great park is a very romantic garden, called Baroucleugh, which consists of seven hanging terrace walks down to the river-side, with a wild wood full of birds on the opposite side of the river. In some of those walks are banqueting-houses, with walks and grottos, and all of them filled with large evergreens in the shape of beasts and birds.

CHAPTER III.

ON CONVENTUAL GARDENS.

POSSIBLY drawings of some Conventual Gardens may yet be found among the papers or chartularies of those families who now inherit some of the splendid monasteries, dissolved by the tasteless and savage tyranny of the monster, the bloody tyrant, Henry; temples erected for the worship of God, 'irresistibly impressing us with solemnity and delight, and which seem intended to rival, in durability, the earth on which they stand, and which, after the lapse of several ages, are still unequalled, not only in point of magnificence of structure, but in their tendency to leave upon the soul the most deep and solemn impressions.' These 'cloud-capp'd towers and solemn temples,' are thus described by poor, deserted, ill-starr'd Chatterton, and Britton has happily quoted his lines as a motto to his most splendid *History of York Cathedral* :—

'What wondrous monument! What pyle ys thys,
That bynds in wonder's chayne entendemente!
That doth aloof the ayrie skyen kiss,
And seemeth mountaynes joyned by cemente,
From Godde hys greete and wondrous storehouse sente.'

The *Encyclopædia of Gardening* notices, at page 88, the attachment which an abbot of Ely, the monks at Edmondsbury, and those at Dunstable, had to their gardens. The same interesting compilation tells us that the extensive orchard of Pitfour contains the ruins of the ancient Abbey of Deer, and its gardens. The Abbey of Rosslyn was built in the middle of a handsome garden. The Caledonian Horticultural Society Memoirs (No. 5) give an interesting notice of the remains of the apple and pear trees, planted by the monks of the Abbey of Lindores; and in Vol. III. of the same work is an account of the Abbey orchards of Melrose, Jedburgh, &c. Orchards, vineyards, and gardens, were the usual appendages to each monastery. We are told that when Stow was young, he collected and amassed MSS. and old records, dispersed by the then recent dissolution, and that such was his avidity in collecting old papers and books,

' *With clasps embossed, and coat of rough bull's hide,*'

that he travelled on foot during the suppression of these religious houses from one part of England to another, collecting records relative to estates, families, &c. It were needless to remark what acquisitions he must have had in his power relative to the gardens of those

' . . . . happy convents, bosom'd deep in vines,
Where slumber'd abbots, purple as their wines.'

Leland, too, had a commission empowering him to search after antiquities, and peruse the libraries of all cathedrals, abbeys, priories, colleges, &c. His voluminous MSS., after passing through many hands, came at last into the Bodleian Library.

CHAPTER IV.

ON GARDEN BURIAL.

SUCH has been the attachment of many to their gardens and to the rural scenes of Nature, that they have expressed a wish to be buried there. Mr. Evelyn expressed the same wish, but was prevailed on to alter it. Sir W. Temple's heart is enclosed in a silver box and buried under a sun-dial in his favourite garden. The late Lord Camelford was so charmed, when travelling through Switzerland, with a rural spot there, that he gave orders in his will to be buried under a tuft of trees which he had marked in that romantic country; and a few years afterwards, when he was shot in a duel near Kensington, his body was accordingly conveyed there. No wonder he was struck with the scenery of that country, when Hirschfeld observes that 'almost all the gardens are theatres of true beauty, without vain ornaments or artificial decorations.' Perhaps his lordship imbibed the soothing wish of Beattie's Minstrel :—

> 'Let vanity adorn the marble tomb
> With trophies, rhymes, and scutcheons of renown,
>   In the deep dungeon of some gothic dome,
> Where night and desolation ever frown.

> Mine be the breezy hill that skirts the down,
> Where a green grassy turf is all I crave,
> With here and there a violet bestrown,
> Fast by a brook or fountain's murmuring wave,
> And many an evening sun shine sweetly on my grave.'

That munificent patron of literature, that worthy and benevolent man, Thomas Hollis, Esq. (Milton's great admirer, and of whom Dr. Franklin observed that 'he loved to do good alone and by stealth'), ordered his body to be buried in one of his fields at Corsham, and the field to be ploughed over immediately after his interment.*

In 1804 the following account is given of his Serene Highness the reigning Duke of Saxe-Gotha: 'He forbade in his will, all ceremony at his burial, except such as is usual for his lowest subjects. He desired to be buried in his English garden, at the feet of the coffins containing the bodies of two of his already deceased children. No speech or sermon to be pronounced, and no monument to be erected over him; but he desires his second son, Prince Frederick, to place a tree upon his grave. To this prince he bequeaths his English garden, which is to be open, as formerly, to all visitors. The simple burial ceremony

---

* Mr. Hollis devoted above half of his large income to deeds of charity. When his house in London was on fire, in 1761, he calmly walked out, only taking under his arm his favourite original picture of Milton.

of this sovereign, took place on the night of the 25th, according to the wish expressed in his will. The reigning Duchess, with her child on her arm, had, the the evening before, strewed flowers round the grave. The midnight hour struck, when the body entered the garden, carried by the servants of the late duke. The walk to the island was laid with black cloth, with the boat that carried it over. The ceremony was only interrupted by the sighs and tears of all present.'

No one delighted more in horticulture and rural affairs than Horne Tooke. Cato, of Utica, could not have exceeded him in this attachment. The intention of Tooke certainly was to have been buried in his own garden, and he had prepared his vault and tomb in his richly cultivated garden at Wimbledon, where both Lord Camelford, and their joint friend, Lord Thurlow,* with other men of rank, who admired his integrity, his overpowering talents, and his genius, were proud to partake of his society. Part of the inscription which he had prepared for that tomb was, that he died 'content and grateful:' satisfied at having lived so long, and gratefully feeling a high sense of the Divine goodness in permitting it; a

* It was said of Lord Thurlow, that he was among lawyers and orators, and in the senate and the courts, what Johnson was among authors and wits: a mighty genius, proudly elevated above the littleness of common minds.

frequent conversation of his being on the wisdom, goodness, and beneficence of the Deity. Horne Tooke was a sincere christian, and closed his long and stormy life ('after having survived the scorpion stings of slander') with an extraordinary degree of calmness and intrepidity. On his decease, however, his friends thought it best to bury him in the grave of his sister at Ealing (at the age of seventy-seven), where the words *content* and *grateful* now form part of the inscription on that stone which covers the remains of that acute scholar, that richly gifted and most' disinterested of men, whose dauntless mind made it his boast, that 'no allurement or threat, no power or oppression, nor life, nor death, thunder or lightning, shall ever force me to give way to corruption or influence, half the breadth of a single hair;' and when enforcing what he deemed beneficial to his country, thus addressed his jury: 'I protest, that if there stood a fire here, and I thought I could by that means affect your minds, and the minds of my countrymen, I would thrust my hand with pleasure into the fire and burn it to ashes, whilst I was pleading before you.' And who, on another occasion, made this declaration: 'I have never committed a single action, nor written a syllable in public or in private, nor entertained a thought (of an important political nature, when taken with all its circumstances of time, place, and occasion), I wish either recalled or concealed; I will die as I have lived, in the commission of the only crime with which I can be charged during my whole life, the crime of speaking *plainly* the *plain* truth.' In the early part of the life of this friendly and kind man, when he resided at Brentford, as a clergyman, no one was more beloved by his parishioners; he administered every possible comfort to the poor; his sermons zealously enforced the excellence of that faith in which he had been educated.

Another person whose talents somewhat remind one of those of Tooke, was also buried in his garden: Theophrastus, who died at the age of eighty-five (though some historians say he wrote his *Characters* when ninety-nine), and whose name was so celebrated throughout Greece, that he had at one time two thousand pupils, lived entirely in his gardens at Athens, to which he was so devoted that, in his will, he left it to some particular friends to study in, and *for the repose of his own bones;* giving orders therein for embellishing the walks, and for the continuation of his old faithful gardener, for whom he had before made a good provision. I will transcribe what a French writer says of him: 'Aristotle charmé de la facilité de son esprit et de la douceur de son élocution, lui changea son nom qui étoit Tyrtaine, en celui *d'Euphraste*, qui signifie celui *qui parle bien*, et ce nom ne répondant point assez à la haute estime qu'il avoit de la beauté de son génie, et de ses expressions, il l'appella *Théophraste*, c'est à dire un homme dont le langage est divin. *Il avoit l'esprit si vif, si perçant, si pénétrant*, qu'il comprenit d'abord, d'une chose, tout ce qui en pouvoit être connu.'

'There is no place' (says Evelyn in his *Sylva*) 'more fit to bury our dead in than groves and gardens, where our beds may be decked and carpeted with verdant and fragrant flowers, trees, and perennial plants, the most natural and instructive hieroglyphics of our resurrection and immortality.' The above remark of Evelyn forcibly reminds one of the following reflections, from a charming little classic book, entitled *First Steps to Botany*, by Dr. Drummond, of Belfast: 'The changes of colour in the leaves of plants, especially of trees, which take place in autumn, are familiar to every one, but are more particularly interesting to the eye of the painter, and the contemplation of the moralist. The one finds in them some of the best subjects for the warmth and beauty of his pencil; the other contrasts these changing leaves with the races of men, which having flourished through the spring and summer of life, fall at last, in the autumn of their existence, into decay, and are swept by the first wintry breath of age into the tomb, and are no more found. Trees have thus been ever considered as emblems of human life, and, in all ages, affecting views and comparisons have been drawn of their progress from debility and infancy to youth, strength, maturity, and inevitable, final decay. The heathen and the atheist have found in them emblems of eternal oblivion, to which they suppose man, with all his high-born hopes, is to be consigned. As the leaves of the tree fall and perish for ever, so *they* represent that when man returns to his mother earth, it is only to mingle with the unthinking material elements; that never more shall he be conscious of existence, and that he, his virtues and his crimes, sink into irrevocable annihilation. Yet as no particle of matter is ever lost, though it may undergo a thousand changes of the most extraordinary kind, so we may rest satisfied that mind is equally indestructible; and though it be impossible for us to trace its flight or modifications after death, there is no reason for a moment to question its future existence, and its immortality. Everything revealed and rational teaches us, that the soul is destined to survive "the wreck of elements and crush of worlds," and that it may go on in increasing knowledge and happiness for ever.'

It is still the custom in many parts, particularly in Guernsey and in Wales, to strew graves with rosemary ('that's for remembrance'), and with the most fragrant flowers the garden produces. It was near Milford Haven that Imogen strewed her supposed husband's grave with 'wild-wood leaves and weeds;' and where Arviragus sweetened the sad grave of Fidele 'with fairest flowers,' asserting that the redbreast would, with its charitable bill, bring all this,

> 'Yea, and furr'd moss besides, when flowers are none,
> To winter-ground thy corse.'

Mr. Cunningham tells us that 'Burns lay in a plain unadorned coffin, with a linen sheet drawn over his face; and on the bed, and around the body, herbs and flowers were thickly strewn, according to the usage of the country.'*

Mr. Carter in his late spirited address, read before the New York Horticultural Society, says: 'Wilson, the distinguished Ornithologist, made a particular request but a few hours before his death, that he might be buried in some rural spot, on the banks of the Schuykill, where the birds might sing over his grave. This sentiment was true to nature; for let philosophy preach as it may, our cares and anxieties, our feelings and affections, will extend to the unconscious dust.'

The following description of an ancient Greek garden is interesting: 'Il est planté de cyprès,

---

* '.... Sepulchrum floribus ornare.'—*Cicero.*

d'ormes, et de peupliers ; les murailles sont tapissées de fleurs qui vont en espaliers, et qui ne demandent pas beaucoup de soin, comme de jasmins, des roses, des chèvre-feuilles, &c. ; le sol est couvert de violettes, et de toutes sortes de fleurs de pris. D'un des angles de ce jardin, il sorte une petite eau courante, qui murmur doucement en faisant plusieurs détours ; elle conserve la fraîcheur de ce beau lieu, où regne un printems éternel ; l'ombre des arbres, le silence et la tranquilité, la variété des fleurs, le murmur du ruisseau, tout donne l'idée de ces champs fortunées où les anciens Grecs croyoient que les âmes vertueuses étoient reçues et récompensées. Ces fleurs sont l'image de cette même vie qui ne dure que l'espace de quelques instans, et qui passent pour ne plus revenir ; car chaque année ramène des fleurs, mais ce ne sont pas celles que nous avons vu fleurir et disparoître.'

Epitaphe.

'Ici repose le corps d'une âme juste, qui n'a jamais cessé de méditer la loi du Seigneur durant sa vie qui a été trop courte. Pendant ce tems, elle a rassasié ceux qui avoient faim, refraîchi ceux qui avoient soif, et couvert ceux qui avoient froid ; elle n'a jamais rien dit qui put affliger personne ; elle a protégé la vertu, et a eu compassion du vicieux ; elle n'a point été attachée aux richesses, et même, a pressa mort, elle les a sacrifiées pour diminuer les peines des autres, autant qu'il a été son pouvoir. Passans, priez pour elle, et imitez-la.'

The celebrated Field-Marshal Loudon, the terror even of Frederick the Great, after the battle of Kunnersdorff, 'l'une des plus meurtrières de toute la guerre' (where Loudon had killed under him 16,000 men, and the king more than 20,000), had so great an attachment to his garden, that his biographer thus relates of him: 'Depuis long tems il avoit choisi, dans son parc à Hadersdorf, un endroit ombragé d'arbres, où il avoit déclaré vouloir être enterré. Il le fit planter d'arbres et de broussailles, et entourer d'une manière fort extraordinaire. Il est vraisemblable qu'il avoit pris ces nouvelles idées des cimetières Turcs, qui sont effectivement remplis d'arbres, car il appelloit ce lieu, ainsi disposé, son jardin Turc. Après la prise de Belgrade, il avoit fait enlever les pierres d'un monument funéraire, on les avoit transportées à Hadersdorf, et il en avoit fait construire un tombeau pour lui-même. Ces pierres ornées d'inscriptions Turques et de guirlandes de fleurs, sont une espèce de marbre blanc. Là git paisiblement M. de Loudon au milieu d'une prairie. Son tombeau est muré et des arbres l'environnent de tous côtés. Ces pierres Turques rappelleront éternellement la prise de Belgrade, et ses victoires sur les fiers Ottomans.'

These fierce Ottomans at Belgrade 'se défendoient en désespérés. Depuis l'invention de la poudre, jamais ville n'avoit essuyé un feu plus terrible. On jeta par milliers dans la place des boulets, des grenades, des bombes, &c. Des témoins oculaires assurent qu'il est impossible de se former une idée du bruit épouvantable que faisoit cette terrible canonade. L'air étoit déchiré par le sifflement des boulets ; la terre trembloit ; l'écho des montagnes retentissoit de coups redoublés et sans cesse renaissans ; la nuit paroissoît aussi claire que le jour, au moyen des flammes dévorantes qui sortoient à chaque instant de tous ces différens instrumens de mort. Le bruit du canon étoit-il un moment suspendu, on entendoit incontinent s'élever de la ville les cris lamentables des infortunés Ottomans.'

Loudon's conflict with Frederick at Prague was equally terrible. 'Un bombardement ruina entièrement cette ville. Le prince vouloit capituler, et demandoit seulement la liberté de se retirer avec les troupes qu'il commandoit. Le roi le refusa; il vouloit avoir complètement le plaisir de faire prisonniers ces 44,000 Autrichiens, ou au moins les rendre inutiles le reste de la guerre. Aussi fit-il tirer sur Prague sans aucun ménagement. Plusieurs milliers de personnes, viellards, femmes et enfans, furent tués par les bombes, ou écrasés dans les maisons qui s'écrouloient. Les Prussiens pouvoient entendre pendant la nuit les cris et les gémissemens de ces infortunés. On mit 12,000 bouches inutiles hors de la ville, afin de prévenir la famine ; mais les Prussiens les y firent rentrer à coups de canon. Pendant les trois premières semaines du siége, la plus grande partie de la ville neuve, et le quartier des juifs furent entièrement brûlés et détruits. On jeta au moins deux cens mille grenades d'obusiers, boulets et bombes dans la ville, qui tuèrent plus de 8000 habitans, et en blessèrent plus de 9000.'

His biographer further relates of him, 'Ce héros, qui avoit essuyé tant de fatigues, affronté tant de périls, mourut dans son lit. Tandis que tant de milliers d'hommes tomboient autour de lui, la mort l'épargna. Monsieur de Loudon, qui à la cour, dans une magnifique salle de gala, se tenoit modestement à l'écart ; qui dans une cercle, ou à une grande table, ne parloit que par monosyllables et sembloit un vrai misanthrope ; qui écoutoit discuter avec une timide modestie la moindre question relative aux sciences ; ce même M. de Loudon à cheval, à la tête d'une armée, paroît être un tout autre homme. Le génie martial le saisit et le métamorphose. Sa voix éclantante se fait entendre à 100,000 guerriers ; chacun se tait lorsqu'il parle ; chaque soldat tremble au moindre de ses gestes. Il est impossible, assurent tous les témoins oculaires, de se faire une idée du feu qui animoit M. de Loudon, lorsqu'on le voyoit à la tête d'une troupe.

Il traversoit, comme un éclair, les rangs et les sections, donnoit ses ordres avec l'impétuosité de la foudre; et malheur à quiconque laissoit appercevoir le moindre signe de désobéissance, de lâcheté, ou d'arrogance. On peut donc appliquer à M. de Loudon le vers suivant:

Est Deus in nobis, agitante calescimus illo.

Un Dieu est en nous, et son action nous échauffe.

En effet, il sembloit que Mars animat notre héros, et qu'il répandit dans son âme son feu divin. Les plus anciens soldats, les généraux les plus aguerris éprouvoient un saisissement respectueux quand M. de Loudon leur donnoit l'ordre du combat.'

CHAPTER V.

ON COTTAGE GARDENS.

WORLIDGE, who wrote about 1680, when speaking on the general attachment for gardens, says, 'Such is its pre-excellency, that there is scarcely a *cottage* in most of the southern parts of England but hath its proportionable garden; so great delight do most men take in it that they may not only please themselves with the view of the flowers, herbs, and trees, as they grow, but furnish themselves and their neighbours upon extraordinary occasions, as nuptials, feasts, and funerals.'

A Mr. Moggridge, of Monmouthshire, communicated to the *Gardener's Magazine*, in January, 1827, respecting the *village gardens* and *cottages* which his compassionate feelings for the poor labourers caused him to establish, 'where seven years ago there was nothing but thickets, brakes, and wood;' but now 'every cottager has his own oven, and bakes his own bread; he has also a corner in his pantry, which I hope to live to see fitted with a small cask of good home-brewed beer or ale; but what is worth both put together—he has his garden. All the villagers' gardens are now well cultivated, some of them highly, producing peas, beans, potatoes, cabbages, cauliflowers, in the vegetable, and more sparingly currants, gooseberries, raspberries, some strawberries, and apples, in the fruit line.' This gentleman has shewn us how very easy it is to add to the comforts of the unoffending hard-labouring poor. His 'village green, of two acres, nearly covered with flourishing oak-trees,' and 'his village, situated in a valley, on ground gently rising from the bank of a romantic mountain river, stretching towards woods, which cover the steeply rising hills,' would have been viewed by Goldsmith with pensive sighs at the recollection of his own *Deserted Village;* and Mr. Gray, or Dr. Watson, the late Bishop of Llandaff, would have travelled miles to have viewed the comfortable abodes of those who had thus been rescued from a state 'bordering on despair,' which absolutely paralysed all the wished-for exertions of their honest labour. This generous advocate for the poor who, one is proud to hear, bears the respectable and commanding title of a magistrate, may well say that what he has thus done carries with it its own reward; and that the hours spent in the consideration how the above might be effected formed 'some of the most interesting of my life.'*

* May the memory of this benevolent gentleman, Mr. Moggridge, receive at a distant course of years the same tribute that has been paid in *Description routine de l'Empire François* to the owner of a

This valuable paper of Moggridge reminds one of the happiness Voltaire experienced when creating his never-to-be-forgotten village of Ferney.'*
The conductor of the above Magazine, after feeling, as so many of his pages indicate he always does, for the comfortless state of too many of our cottage labourers, observes that 'there are few ways in which a landed proprietor could do more good to society, or lay a more solid foundation for self-satisfaction;' and the same gentleman at page 1027 of his *Encyclopædia of Gardening* observes that 'whatever renders the

sweet village between Moulins and Lyons through which Petrarch, and later Sterne, must often have passed. 'Chaseuille, village qu'on traverse une demi-lieue avant Varennes. Au milieu de l'amphithéâtre de verdure qu'ils déploient aux regards enchantés du voyageur, s'élève parmi les pampres, les vergers et les bosquets, le château seigneurial du village : aussi simple par sa structure que délicieux par sa situation, il n'étale ni pavillons voluptueux, ni tours menaçantes ; il commande moins le village qu'il ne l'embellit. Cette aimable et modeste habitation est celle d'un vieillard philantrope, M. de Chaseuille, qui, persuadé que les seigneurs de la terre, comme celui du ciel, ne doivent manifester leur pouvoir aux hommes que par le bien qu'ils leur font, avait trouvé le secret de se faire adorer de ses vassaux. Il est douloureux de penser que ce vieux ami des hommes n'existe peut-être plus au moment de la publication de cet ouvrage (il était à la fin de sa carrière) ; nous aurons du moins la consolation d'avoir jeté quelques fleurs sur sa tombe.'

* I am informed that the room at Ferney from whence issued some of the brightest emanations of Voltaire, is now actually the room where boots and shoes are cleaned.

cottager more comfortable and happy at home will render him a better servant and subject, and in every respect a more valuable member of society. Besides one of the most constantly occurring objects in the country is the labourer's cottage, whether detached by the roadside or grouped in hamlets and villages, and, therefore, to render such buildings and their scenery more ornamental must, independently of every other consideration, be a very laudable object;' and again at page 1044 he observes, 'It would be a most desirable circumstance if proprietors who keep head-gardeners would desire them to attend to the gardens of the cottagers on their estates, to supply them with proper seeds and plants; to propagate for them a few fruit-trees, and distribute them in the proper place in their plots; to teach them modes of culture suitable for their circumstances. In this way, at no additional expense whatever to the proprietor, much happiness might be diffused; and constantly recurring objects, too often indicating wretchedness or, at least, slovenliness, rendered useful, neat, and even ornamental.'

Lord Gardenstone in his Memorandums concerning the village of Lawrence Kirk inserted in the *European Magazine*, declares, 'I felt an agreeable zeal in the project, and contracted a fond affection to the people as they became inhabitants of my village. I have tried in some measure a variety of pleasures which mankind pursue, but never relished any so much as the pleasure arising from the progress of my village.'

W. Mavor, in his edition of *Tusser*, makes this observation: 'Bind the poor man by his interest as well as his duty to the place where he lives, and he will feel the pride of deserving well.'

One hopes, and believes, that the following strong language of Nourse, in his *Campania Fœlix*, printed in 1700, applied then (as it may do now) to very few: 'We may take leave to glance a little at the behaviour of some Lords of Manors, whose bailiffs many times wheedle in the cottagers, allowing them liberty to build upon the waste, and to inclose ground perhaps; giving them a tree or two to carry on the design, upon condition they will take a lease of such cottages for three lives, paying only some sixpenny rent; upon the expiration of which term, his hungry lordship swallows the poor cottage, with all its members and dependences, at a bit, which, by the sweat and labour of the poor defunct and his predecessors, was improved to a kind of competency out of nothing, whilst the remains of the poor family are exposed to the naked world, or else forced to pay a good round fine for the renewal of that which was so dearly purchased by their own pains and industry; by which sly methods, the commonage will be engrossed in time, and many whole families be devoured, to serve the appetite of an insatiable patron.'

W. Withers, of Holt, in his late letter to Sir W. Scott, forcibly remarks: 'Here, Sir Walter, I feel the want of your pen, to enable me to appeal with effect to the great landed proprietors, and to prove to them, how closely their interests are bound up with the welfare of the labouring classes; to show how much more it would be to their advantage to be surrounded by industrious, well-fed, happy, and contented labourers, devoted to their interests, rather than have their estates encumbered by idle, half-starved, discontented paupers, and frequently engaged in acts of plunder and violence, and ripe, at all times, to avail themselves of any opportunity for wreaking their vengeance upon those, whom, under other circumstances, they would sacrifice their lives to protect. This is no exaggerated picture of the condition and feelings of the majority of the labouring classes, no supposititious or imaginary evil, no chimerical or false notion; but a real, palpable, existing, and notorious deformity in the present state of society. I have opportunities of knowing, and I do know, the feelings of the labouring classes towards their employers and superiors; and I have no hesitation in saying that, bad as is their condition, though they have suffered much, and have but too frequently been ill-used, nothing is wanting but remunerating wages, good living, and kind treatment, to bring them back to those honest, industrious, and obedient habits, for which their forefathers in the same situation of life were distinguished.'

I need make no apology to my reader for inserting *The Funeral Oration of a Peasant*, from the pen of the celebrated Monsieur Mercier: 'Passing by a village, I saw a company of peasants, their eyes dejected and wet with tears, who were entering a temple. The sight struck me; I ordered the carriage to stop, and followed them in. I saw in the middle of the temple the corpse of an old man, in the habit of a peasant, whose white hairs hung down to the ground. The pastor of the village mounted a small eminence, and said, "My fellow-countrymen, the man you here see was for ninety years a benefactor to mankind. He was the son of a husbandman, and in his infancy his feeble hands attempted to guide the plough. As soon as his legs could support him, he followed his father in the furrows. When years had given him that strength for which he long wished, he said to his father, 'Cease from your labours;' and from that time each rising sun has seen him till the ground, sow, plant, and reap the harvest. He has cultivated more than two thousand acres of fresh land. He has planted the vine in all the country round about; and to him you owe the fruit-trees that nourish your village, and afford you shelter from the sun. It was not avarice that made him unwearied in his labours; no, it was the love of industry, for which he was wont to say, man was born; and the great and sacred belief that God regarded him when cultivating his lands for the nourishment of his children. He married and had twenty-five children. He formed them all to labour and to virtue, and they have all maintained an unblemished character. He has taken care to marry them properly, and led them, with a smiling aspect, to the altar. All his grandchildren have been brought up in his house; and you know what a pure unalterable joy dwells upon their countenances. All these brethren love one another, because he loved them, and made them see what pleasure he found in loving them. On days of rejoicing, he was the first to sound the rural instruments; and his looks, his voice, and gesture, you know, were the signals for universal mirth. You cannot but remember his gaiety, the lively effect of a peaceful mind, and his speeches full of sense and wit; for he had the gift of exercising an ingenious raillery without giving offence. He cherished order from an eternal sense he had of virtue. Whom has he ever refused to serve? When did he show himself unconcerned at public or private misfortunes? When was he indifferent in his country's cause? His heart was devoted to it; in his conversation he constantly wished for its prosperity. When age had bent his body, and his legs trembled under him, you have seen him mount to the summit of a hill, and give lessons of experience to the young husbandmen. His memory was the faithful depository of observations, made during the course of fourscore successive years, on the changes of the several seasons. Such a tree, planted by his hand in such a year, recalled to his memory the favour or the wrath of heaven. He had by heart what other men forget—the fruitful harvests, the deaths and legacies to the poor. He seemed to be endowed with a prophetic spirit, and when he meditated by the light of the moon, he knew with what seeds to enrich his garden. The evening before his death he said, 'My children, I am drawing nigh to that Being who is the author of all good, whom I have always adored, and in whom I trust. To-morrow prune your pear-trees, and at the setting of the sun, bury me at the head of my grounds.' You are now, children, going to place him there, and ought to imitate his example; but, before you inter these white hairs, which have so long attracted respect, behold with reverence his hardened hands; behold the honourable marks of his long labours."

The orator then held up one of his cold hands; it had acquired twice the usual size by continual labour, and seemed to be invulnerable to the point of the briar, or the edges of the flint; he then respectfully kissed the hand, and all the company followed his example. His children bore him to the grave on three sheaves of corn, and buried him as he had desired, placing on his grave his hedging-bill, his spade, and a ploughshare. "Ah!" I cried, "if those men, celebrated by Bossuet, Flechier, Mascaron, and Neuville, had the hundredth part of the virtue of this villager, I would pardon them their pompous and futile eloquence."'

CHAPTER VI.

ON THE CULTIVATION OF THE VINE IN ENGLAND.

From 'The whole Art of Husbandry,' enlarged by Barnaby Googe, 4to. black letter, 1614. The first edition was published in 1577. This curious book is by way of dialogue.

MARIUS.—You heare my wife calleth us to supper, and you see the shadow is ten foote long, therefore, it is high time we goe.

Thra.—I give you most harty thankes that you have thus friendly entertained mee in this your fayre orchard, with the sweet description of these pleasant hearbes and trees.

Julia.—Sir, your supper is ready, I pray you make an end of your talke, and let the gentleman come in heere into this arbour.

Another short extract will show the nature of this book: 'Epicure is reported to be the first that euer deuised gardens in Athens, before his time it was not seene, that the pleasures of the countrie were had in the citie. Now when Thrasybulus trauailing in the affayres of his prince, chaunced to come to the house of Marius, and carried by him into a garden that he had, which was very beautifull, being led about among the sweet smelling flowres, and vnder the pleasant arbours, what a goodly sight (quoth Thrasybulus) is heere. how excellently haue you garnished this paradise of yours with all kinde of pleasures. Your parlers, and your banketting houses both within and without, as all bedecked with pictures of beautifull flowres and trees, that you may not onely feede your eyes with the beholding of the true and liuely flowre, but also delight your selfe with the counterfait in the midst of winter, seeing in the one, the painted flower to contend in beautie with the very flower: in the other, the wonderfull worke of nature, and in both, the passing goodness of God. Moreouer, your pleasant arbours to walke in, whose shaddowes keepe off the heate of the sunne, and if it fortune to raine, the cloisters are hard by. But specially this little riuer, with most cleere water, encompassing the garden, doth wonderfully set it forth, and herewithall the greene and goodly quickset hedges.'

In his *Dedication* he observes that 'there is, in my fancie, no life so quiet, so acceptable to God, and pleasant to an honest minde, as is the life of the countrie, where a man, withdrawing himselfe from the miseries, vanities, and vexations of this foolish and now too too much doting world, may giue himselfe to the sweet contemplation of God, and his workes, and the profit and reliefe of his poore distressed neighbour, to which two things we were chiefely created, I thought it good to send you here (as a token and a testimonie of my thankfull mind, for your sundry friendships and curtesies shewed vnto me) a rude draught of the order and manner of the said countrie life, which you may vse (if it please you) for your recreation. And afterwards (if so you thinke it meet) publish vnder your protection, to the commoditie and benefit of others. Fare you well: from Kingstone.'

In his epistle to the reader he thus speaks of the Cultivation of the Vine: 'I am fully perswaded if diligence, and good husbandrie might be vsed, wee might haue a reasonable good wine growing in many places of this realme: as vndoubtedly we had immediately after the Conquest, till partly by slothfulnesse not liking any thing long that is painefull, partly by ciuill discord long continuing it was left, and so with time lost, as appeareth by a number of places in this realme, that keepes still the name of vineyards: and vpon many cliffes and hilles are yet to be seene the rootes, and olde remaines of vines. There is besides *Notingham* an auncient house called *Chilwell*, in vvhich house remaineth yet as an auncient monument in a great vvindow of glasse, the whole order of planting, proyning, stamping, and pressing of vines. Besides, there is yet also growing an olde vine that yeelds a grape sufficient to make a right good wine, as vvas lately proved by a gentlewoman in the sayd house. There hath moreouer good experience of late yeeres beene made, by two noble and honourable Barons of this realme, the *Lord Villiams of Tame*, and the *Lord Cobham*, vvho both had growing about their houses as good vines, as are in many places of France. And if they answere not in all points euery mans expectation, the fault is rather to be imputed to the malice and disdaine peraduenture of the Frenchmen that kept them, then to any ill disposition, or fault of the soyle. For vvhere haue you in any place better, or pleasanter Wines, then about *Backrach, Colin, Andernach*, and diuers other places of Germanie, that haue in manner the selfe-same latitude and disposition of the heauens that we haue? Beside, that the nearenesse to the south, is not altogether the causer of good wines, appeareth in that you haue about *Orleans*, great store of good and excellent wine: whereas, if you goe to *Burges*, two dayes iourney farther to the south, you shall finde a wine not worth the drinking. The like is (as I haue heard reported by Master D. Dale, Embassadour for his Maiestie in these parts) of *Paris* and *Barleduke*, the towne being southward, vvith noughtie wines; the other a great wayes farther to the north, vvith as good wines as may be. But admit England would yeeld none so strong and pleasant wines as are desired (as I am fully perswaded it would) yet it is worth the triall and trauaile to haue wines of our owne, though they be the smaller: and therefore I thought it not meet to leaue out of my booke the ordering and trimming of vines.'*

* Much curious information on our English vineyards may be seen in the *Encyclopædia of Gardening*, under the article 'Grape Vine.'

CHAPTER VII.

MR. POPE'S LETTER TO MARTHA BLOUNT,

*Describing the seat of Sir W. Raleigh.**

I PROMISED you an account of Sherborne before I had seen it, or knew what I undertook. I imagined it to be one of those fine old seats of which there are numbers scattered over England. But this is so peculiar, and its situation of so uncommon a kind that it merits a more particular description. The house is in the form of an **H**. The body of it, which was built by Sir Walter Raleigh,

---

* In the note to the first page of the Preface to this present volume, a brief description is given of Sir W. Raleigh's seat and garden, which I copied from Coker's *Survey of Dorset*. A more modern description of that seat appears in the above letter of Pope's. In one of Digby's letters to Pope, he mentions his frequent meditations in Raleigh's grove. Sir Walter's predilection for gardens, and for the choice and curious productions of nature, appears in many instances. Gerard dedicates the second edition of his list of his own garden in Holborn, to his patron, Sir W. Raleigh. Sir Walter married a daughter of Sir Nicholas Carew, of Beddington, the gardens of which were much celebrated in the sixteenth century. In Hutchin's *History and Antiquities of Sherbourne*, augmented and continued to the present time, by R. Gough and J. B. Nichols, are given some particulars of this estate and some very curious ones respecting Sir Walter. Aubrey, in his *Diary*, speaking of Sherbourne says:

consists of four stories, with four six-angled towers at the ends. These have since been joined to four wings, with a regular stone balustrade at the top, and four towers more that finish the building. The windows and gates are of a yellow stone throughout; and one of the flat sides towards the garden has the wings of a newer architecture, with beautiful Italian window

' In short, and indeed, 'tis a most sweet and pleasant place, and scite, as any in the west, perhaps none like it.' And he further says, ' The time of his execution was contrived to be on my Lord Mayor's day, that the pageantes and fine shewes might drawe away the people from beholding the tragedie of one of the gallantest worthies that England ever bred.' Dr. Tounson says, ' He was the most fearless of death that ever was known.' In St. Margaret's, Westminster, is this inscription : ' Within the walls of this church were deposited the body of the great Sir W. Raleigh, on the day he was beheaded in Old Palace Yard, 18 October, 1618.' When Sir Walter was confined at Winchester, in daily expectation of death, he wrote a letter to his wife, (the daughter of the above-mentioned Sir Nicholas Carew), and the following is part of that letter :—' You shall receive, my dear wife, my last words in these my last lines; my love I send you, that you may keep when I am dead ; and my counsel, that you may remember it when I am no more. I would not with my will present you sorrows ; dear Bess, let them go to the grave with me, and be buried in the dust. And seeing that it is the will of God, that I should not see you any more, bear my destruction patiently, and with an heart like yourself. First, I send you all the thanks which heart can conceive, or my words express, for your many travels and cares for me, which, though they have not taken effect as you wished, yet my debt to you is not the less ; but pay it I never shall in this world. Secondly, I beseech you, for the love you bear me living, that you do not hide yourself many days, but by your travels seek to help my miserable frames, done by the first Earl of Bristol, which, if they were joined in the middle by a portico covering the old building, would be a noble front. The design of such an one I have been amusing myself with drawing; but it is a question whether Lord Digby will not be better amused than to execute it. The finest room is a saloon, fifty feet long, and a parlour

fortunes, and the sight of your poor child; your mourning cannot avail me that am but dust. I trust my blood will quench their malice who desired my slaughter, that they will not seek also to kill you and your's with extreme poverty. To what friend to direct you I know not; for all mine have left me in the true time of trial. Most sorry am I, that being thus surprised by death, I can leave you no better estate. God hath prevented all my determinations; that great God that worketh all in all. And if you can live free from want, care for no more, for the rest is but vanity. Remember your poor child for his father's sake, who loved you in his happiest estate. I sued for my life, but (God knows) it was for you and your's that I desired it; for know it, my dear wife, your child is the child of a true man, who, in his own respect, despised death and his mis-shapen and ugly forms. I cannot write much. God knows how hardly I steal this time when all are asleep; and it is also time for me to separate my thoughts from the world. Beg my dead body, which living was denied you, and either lay it in Sherburn, or in Exeter Church, by my father and mother. Time and death calleth me away. The everlasting God, powerful, infinite, and inscrutable God Almighty, who is goodness itself, the true light and life, keep you and your's, and have mercy upon me, and forgive my persecutors and false accusers, and send us to meet in his glorious kingdom. My dear wife, farewell. Bless my boy, pray for me, and let my true God hold you both in his arms. Your's that was, but now not my own, *Walter Raleigh.*'

hung with very excellent tapestry of Rubens, which was a present from the King of Spain to the Earl of Bristol in his embassy there. This stands in a park finely crowned with very high woods on all the tops of the hills, which form a great amphitheatre sloping down to the house. On the garden sides the woods approach close, so that it appears there with a thick line and depth of groves on each hand, and so it shows from most parts of the park. The gardens are so irregular that it is very hard to give an exact idea of them but by a plan. Their beauty arises from this irregularity; for not only the several parts of the garden itself make the better contrast by these sudden rises, falls, and turns of the ground, but the views about are let in and hang over the walls in very different figures and aspects. You come first out of the house into a green walk of standard limes, with a hedge behind them that makes a colonnade; hence into a little triangular wilderness, from whose centre you see the town of Sherborne in a valley interspersed with trees. From the corner of this you issue at once upon a high green terrace, the whole breadth of the garden, which has five more green terraces hanging under each other, without hedges, only a few pyramid yews and large round honeysuckles between them. The honeysuckles hereabouts are the largest and finest I ever saw. You'll be pleased when I tell you the quarters of the above-mentioned little wilderness are filled with these and with cherry-trees of the best kinds, all within reach of the hand. At the ends of these terraces run two long walks under the side-walls of the garden which communicate with the other terraces that front these opposite. Between the valley is laid level, and divided into two irregular groves of horse-chestnuts and a bowling-green in the middle of about 180 feet. This is bounded behind with a canal that runs quite across the groves, and also along one side in the form of a T. Behind this is a semicircular *berceau*, and a thicket of mixed trees that completes the crown of the amphitheatre, which is of equal extent with the bowling-green. Beyond that runs a natural river through green banks of turf, over which rises another row of terraces, the first supported by a slope wall, planted with vines; so is also the wall that bounds the channel of the river. A second and third appeared above this; but they are to be turned into a line of wilderness, with wild winding walks, for the convenience of passing from one side to the other in shade; the heads of whose trees will lie below the uppermost terrace of all, which completes the garden and overlooks both that and the country. Even above the wall of this the natural ground rises and is crowned with several venerable ruins of an old castle, with arches and broken views of which I must say more hereafter. When you are at the left corner of the canal, and the chestnut groves in the bottom, you turn of a sudden, under very old trees, into the deepest shade. The walk winds you up a hill of venerable wood, over-arched by nature and of a vast height, into a circular grove, on one side of which is a close high arbour, on the other a sudden open seat that overlooks the meadows and river with a large distant prospect. Another walk under this hill winds by the river-side, quite covered with high trees on both banks, over-hung with ivy, where falls a natural cascade with never-ceasing murmurs. On the opposite hanging of the bank (which is a steep of fifty feet) is placed, with a very fine fancy, a rustic seat of stone, flagged and rough, with two urns in the same rude taste, upon pedestals, on each side, from whence you lose your eyes upon the glimmering of the waters under the wood, and your ears in the constant dashing of the waves. In view of this is a bridge that crosses this stream, built in the same ruinous taste; the wall of the garden hanging over it is humoured so as to appear the ruin of another arch or two above the bridge. Hence you mount the hill, over the hermit's seat (as they call it), described before, and so to the highest terrace again. On the left, full behind these old trees which make this whole part inexpressibly awful and solemn, runs a little, old, low wall, beside a trench covered with elder trees and ivy; which, being crossed by another bridge, brings you to the ruins, to complete the solemnity of the scene. You first see an old tower, penetrated by a large arch and others above it, through which the whole country appears in prospect, even when you are at the top of the other ruins; for they stand very high, and the ground slopes down on all sides. These venerable broken walls, some arches almost entire, of thirty or forty feet deep, some open like porticoes with fragments of pillars, some circular or enclosed on three sides but exposed at top, with steps, which time has made of disjointed stones to climb to the highest points of the ruin. These, I say, might have a prodigious beauty, mixed with greens and parterres from part to part, and the whole heap standing as it does on a round hill kept smooth in green turf, which makes a bold basement to show it. The open courts from building to building might be thrown into circles or octagons of grass or flowers; and even in the gaping rooms you have fine trees grown that might be made a natural tapestry to the walls, and arch you overhead where time has uncovered them to the sky. Little paths of earth or sand might be made up the half-tumbled walls to guide from one view to another on the higher parts; and seats placed here and there to enjoy those views, which are more romantic than imagination can form them. I could very much wish this were done, as well as a little temple built on a neighbouring round hill that is seen from all points of the garden and is extremely pretty. It would finish some walks, and particularly be a fine termination to the river and be seen from the entrance into that deep scene I have described by the cascade, where it would appear as in the clouds, between the tops of some very lofty trees that form an arch before it, with a great slope downward to the end of the said river.

CHAPTER VIII.

POPE'S VILLA AT TWICKENHAM.

Now the residence of the Right Honourable Wellebore Ellis, 1789. From the 'Topographer.'*

OF all the villages situated on the banks of the Thames, Twickenham is acknowledged to be one of the most pleasant. Its vicinity to the metropolis, its fine prospect of the river, and the enchanting view of perhaps the richest landscapes in England, have, of late years, made it the centre of wealth and fashion, and at the distance of more than half a century ago captivated the taste, and procured it to the residence of one of the most elegant and harmonious of our poets. With the same veneration that a true Mussulman makes a pilgrimage to the tomb of his prophet, a lover of the Muses visits that hallowed spot where the last notes were echoed from the lyre of Pope! So

---

* Brewer, in the *Beauties of England and Wales*, most feelingly relates the devastation committed on this spot a few years since, which 'the bright sunshine of intellect once illumined.' One may apply to Mr. Pope the line which Shakespeare addressed to Anne Hathaway :—

'*Thy eternal summer shall not fade.*'

forcibly indeed has this passion operated that the neighbourhood is no less indebted for its population than its celebrity to this circumstance. Of all the nations in Europe, the English have the greatest attachment to *classic* ground. The genius of improvement has been called in to aid the natural advantages of this charming place, for the present possessor has not only expended a considerable sum of money in the extension, but has also been at infinite pains in the adorning of the grounds, which must now be allowed to exhibit some of the sweetest portions of cultivated scenery in the vicinity of the capital. In the lifetime of the poetical architect, the house, like his own ambition, was humble and confined; since that period attachment to his memory has enlarged its dimensions and made it in some measure worthy of his virtues. The centre building only was inhabited by Pope. Sir William Stanhope, his successor, added two wings, and considerably enlarged the garden adjoining to it, circumstances which he has recorded on a marble tablet placed above an arch leading to his new acquisitions:

> 'The humble roof, the garden's scanty line,
> Ill suit the genius of a bard divine;
> But fancy now displays a fairer scope,
> And Stanhope's plans unfold the soul of Pope.'

Mr. Ellis has stuccoed the front of the house and

fitted it up in an elegant and even magnificent style; the rooms are lofty and of large dimensions; the furniture, which is modern, is of the most costly workmanship, and the pictures at once display the taste and the opulence of the owner. A charming greenhouse, a cold bath, a succession house, and a pinery, have also been added by that gentleman. The lawn, which was formerly a narrow grass plot, has, within these few months, been enlarged by late purchases from the executors of the Honourable Mr. Shirley; it runs now almost the whole length of Cross Deep, and being embanked at the bottom, forms a beautiful inflection parallel to the curve of the river. The top of it is fashioned into a noble terrace several hundred feet in length, from whence Richmond Hill is seen rising like a verdant amphitheatre, out of the bottom of a country finely diversified with wood. The slope which declines gently towards the Thames exhibits a charming and romantic prospect of that noble river, the face of which is ever varying by the continual and uninterrupted succession of objects that float upon its surface. Meandering walks, everywhere shadowed with flowering shrubs and evergreens, afford a cool and agreeable shelter from the scorching rays of the summer's sun, and being peopled by sylvan choristers, who sport here undisturbed, add not a little to the fascinating enjoyments of a situation that at once unites beauty and harmony. Towards the margin of the stream, propped with uncommon care, and guarded by a holy zeal from the ravages of time, still stands the *Weeping Willow*, planted by the hand of 'The Bard of Twickenham.' From this a thousand slips are annually transmitted to the most distant quarters of the globe, and during the present year the Empress of Russia has planted some in her own garden at St. Petersburg. Underneath this tree a small band of instrumental music is stationed during the summer, the melody of which, by the intervention of the water, has a charming effect. The *grotto*, once so celebrated, is now only remarkable by having been erected under the eye of its classical composer. The dilapidations of time, and *pious thefts* of travellers, who select the spars, ores, and even the common flints as so many *holy relics*, have brought it nearly to decay. It no longer forms a 'camera obscura,' nor does 'the thin alabaster lamp of an orbicular form' now 'irradiate the star of looking-glass' placed in the centre of it. Even 'the perpetual rill that echoed through the garden night and day' is no longer in existence. The thirsty Naiads placed round its basin, which still remain, pant for their native element and lament their empty urns! In two adjoining apertures in the rock, a *Ceres* and a *Bacchus*, an excellent bust of Pope, and some other figures are placed, one of which has a *cockle-shell* in the fore part of the hat, after the manner of the ancient pilgrims. The right-hand cavity, which opens to the river by means of a small window latticed with iron bars, it is said contained the Poet when he composed some of his happiest verses. It is impossible to leave this subterraneous abode without a sympathetic recollection of the following apposite lines:—

'. . . . lo ! th' Egerian grot
Where nobly pensive St. John sat and thought,
Where British sighs from dying Wyndham stole,
And the bright flame was shot through Marchmont's soul.'

At the extremity, next the garden, is an inscription cut on white marble:—

'*Secretum Iter
Et Fallentis semita Vitæ.*'

In another grotto which passes under a road to the stables, and connects the pleasure grounds, there are three beautiful busts of Sir W. Stanhope, his daughter, and the late Lord Chesterfield, cut in Italian marble; opposite each a Roman urn of exquisite workmanship is placed in a niche formed in the wall; around are scattered huge masses of stone in imitation of rocks; wild plants and hardy forest trees that delight in bleak situations are also planted on each side to give a sylvan rudeness to the scene. From this, after visiting the orangery, &c., &c., the stranger is led to a small obelisk erected by Pope to the memory of his mother. On the base of it is the following motto, at once descriptive of the piety of the son and the virtue of the mother :—

> '*Ah! Editha*
> *Matrum Optima,*
> *Mulierum Amantissima,*
> *Vale!*'

The groves around it, which are of a circular form, lead into each other by means of narrow alleys; the whole is in the taste of Queen Anne's reign, and in regard to the design, remains exactly as when first planted. Notwithstanding the uniformity of the ground plan, it must be acknowledged that the cypress, yew, and laurel, with which this part of the pleasure grounds abound, are planted in such a manner as to give a more mournful and expressive appearance to the scene than could have been easily achieved by all the boasted effects of modern gardening.

LIST OF BOOKS & VIEWS REFERRED TO.

                                                                PAGE

ADDISON (Joseph), Biographical Sketch of, ... 16
[See] Drake (N.). Essays, &c. Vol. 1.

ADDISON (Right Hon. J.). Miscellaneous works . . . of J. J. . . . with some account of the life and writings of the author, by Mr. Tickell 16
        London. 1736. 8vo.
  Another ed.   ,,   1746. 8vo.
  ,, ,, ,,   1766. 12mo.
  ,, ,, ,,   1777. 12mo.

ADDISON (Right Hon. J.), Works of. [With a preface by Thomas Tickell] 16
        London. 1722. 12mo.
  Another ed.   ,,   1804. 8vo.
  ,, ,, ,,   1811. 8vo.

AGGAS (Ralph). Oxonia Antiqua Instaurata, sive Urbis et Academiæ Oxoniensis topographica delineatio, olim a Radulpho Agas impressa A.D. 1578, nunc denuo æri incisa. 2 tab. 1728 . . . .

ATKYNS (Sir R.). The Ancient and present state of Glostershire.
        London. 1712. Fol.
  Second ed.   ,,   1768. Fol.

AUBREY (John). Diary 88

AUBREY (John). Lives of Eminent Men. Letters written by eminent persons in the seventeenth and eighteenth centuries, &c. Vol. 2, pt. 1. 1813. 8vo. 14

AUBREY (John). The natural history and antiquities of the county of Surrey. 5 Vols. London, 1717-18-19. 8vo. . 8

		PAGE
BADESLADE (T.) [*See*] Kent	. . . .	7

BEATTIE (James). The Minstrel, or, the Progress of Genius;
a poem. 60
    London. 1771. 4to.
 Second ed. ,, 1774. 4to.
 And numerous editions to 1851.

BEAUTIES OF ENGLAND AND WALES 9
 [*See*] Brayley (E. W.) and Britton (J.)

BEEVERELL (J.). Delices de la Grande Bretagne et de l'Irlande.
    8 tom. Leide. 1707. 8vo.   5 & 7
 Nouvelle ed. ,, ,, 1727. 8vo.

BRADLEY (Richard). New Improvements of Planting and
 Gardening. 19
    London. 1717. 8vo.
 2nd ed. 3 pt. ,, 1718. 8vo.
 3rd ed. 3 pt. ,, 1719–20. 8vo.
 4th ed. 5 pt. ,, 1724. 8vo.
 5th ed. 3 pt. ,, 1726. 8vo.
 6th ed. 2 pt. ,, 1731. 8vo.
 7th ed.   ,, 1739. 8vo.

BRAY (William). Memoirs, illustrative of the life and writings
of John Evelyn, comprising his Diary . . . 1641-1705-6.
Edited by W. Bray. 3
    London. 1818. 4to.
 2 Vols. ,, 1819. 4to.
 4 ,, ,, 1850–52. 8vo.

BRAYLEY (Edward Wedlake) and BRITTON (John). The Beauties
 of England and Wales. 18 Vols. in 26 . . . .
    London. 1801–15. 8vo.
 [First six volumes by Brayley and Britton; remaining
  volumes by various authors.]

BRIDGEMAN (Sarah) 8
 [*See*] Stowe, co. Bucks. A general plan, &c.

BRITANNIA ILLUSTRATA; or, views, &c. 7
 2 vols. London. 1720–40. Fol.

BIBLIOGRAPHY. 105

BRITTON (John). Architectural Antiquities of Great Britain. xiv. & 1
5 vols. London. 1807-27. 4to.
Vol. 5 has a second title-page, which reads: 'Chronological history ... of Christian Architecture,' &c.

BRITTON (John). An historical and architectural essay relating to Redcliffe Church, Bristol, ... also an essay on the life and character of T. Chatterton. London. 1813. 8vo.   xiii & 9

BRITTON (John). The history and antiquities of the Metropolitical Church of York, illustrated, &c. London. 1819. 4to.   57

BUCK (Samuel) and (Nathanael). [A collection of engravings of castles, abbeys, and towns in England and Wales, by S. and N. B., afterwards republished under the title of Buck's Antiquities.] 5 vols. [London.] 1721-52. Obl. fol.   .   4

BURGHER (Michael). [See] Plot (R.)   9

BURTON (William). The description of Leicestershire.   .   .   6
London. [1622.] Fol.
2nd ed. Lynn. 1777. Fol.

CALEDONIAN HORTICULTURAL SOCIETY. Memoirs, &c.   .   .   58
Vol. 1-4, 5; pt. 1. Edinburgh. 1814-32. 8vo.
No more of Vol. 5 published.

CAUX (Isaac de). [See] Wilton, in Wiltshire   7

CHATELAIN (M.)   8
[See] Stowe, co. Bucks. Sixteen Perspective Views.

CHATTERTON (Thomas). [See] Britton (John)   .   xiii & xiv

CHAUNCEY (Sir Henry). The historical Antiquities of Hertfordshire. London. 1700. Fol.   2
Another ed. 2 vols. Bishops Stortford. 1826. 8vo.

CHISWICK. Six views of the Earl of Burlington's Seat at Chiswick, by Donowell. 1753.   8

CHISWICK. Two views of the Earl of Burlington's Seat at Chiswick, by Rysbrake.   8

BIBLIOGRAPHY.

PAGE

COBBETT (William). The English Gardener; or, a treatise on
... kitchen gardens ... hot beds, greenhouses, &c. . 20
London. 1829. 12mo.

COBBETT (William). Rural Rides in the Counties of Surrey,
Kent, Sussex, Hampshire, &c. vii
    London. 1830. 12mo.
New ed.   ,, 1853. 12mo.
New ed.   ,, 1885. 8vo.

COBBETT (William). The Woodlands: or, a treatise ... on
the planting, on the cultivating ... of Forest trees and
Underwoods, &c. London. 1825. 8vo. 19

COKER (John). A Survey of Dorsetshire. London. 1732. Fol. 88

CRÈVECŒUR (Michael Guillaume Jean de). Letters from an
American Farmer. viii
    London. 1782. 8vo.
Another ed. Dublin. 1782. 12mo.
,, ,, Belfast. 1783. 12mo.

DALLAWAY (James). Anecdotes of the Arts in England . . 5
    London. 1800. 8vo.
Another ed.   ,, 1800. 4to.

DALLAWAY (James). Supplementary Anecdotes of Gardening. 21
[See] Walpole (Horace). Anecdotes of Painting.

DEFOE (Daniel). A Tour thro' the whole Island of Great Britain. 28
 3 vols. London. 1724. 8vo.
Another ed.   ,, 1742. 12mo.
,, ,,   ,, 1748. 12mo.
,, ,,   ,, 1753. 12mo.
,, ,, 4 vols. ,, 1769. 12mo.
,, ,, ,, ,, 1778. 8vo.

DEFOE (Daniel). A Journey through England and Scotland.
3 vols. 1714 28

DESCRIPTION ROUTINE DE L'EMPIRE FRANÇOIS. . . . 74

DIGBY (R.). Letters to (A.) Pope. [See] Pope (A.) Letters, &c. 88

BIBLIOGRAPHY.   107

DILLENIUS (Joannes Jacobus). Hortus Elthamensis, seu Plantarum rariorum, quas in horto suo Elthami in Cantio coluit ... J. Sherard Gulielmi p.m. frater, delineationes et descriptiones. 2 vols. Londini. 1732. Folio . . . 24
Another copy with *Coloured Plates.*

DONOWELL ( ). [*See*] Chiswick. Six Views, &c. . . . 8

DRAKE (Nathan) M.D. Essays, Biographical, Critical, and Historical, Illustrative of the *Tatler, Spectator,* and *Guardian.* 3 vols. London. 1805. 8vo. 16

DRAKE (Nathan), M.D. Mornings in Spring. 2 vols. London. 1828. 8vo. 13

DRUMMOND (James L.). First Steps to Botany. . . . 65
         London. 1823. 12mo.
2nd ed.   ,,   1826. 12mo.
4th ed.   ,,   1835. 12mo.

DUGDALE (Sir William). The Antiquities of Warwickshire . 3
         London. 1656. Fol.
2nd ed. 2 vols.   ,,   1730. Fol.
Another ed.   Coventry. 1765. Fol.

EUROPEAN MAGAZINE. 87 vols. London. 1782-1825. 8vo. 76
New Series. Vols. 1, 2. London. 1825-26. 8vo.

EVELYN (Charles). The Lady's Recreation; or, the Art of Gardening further improved 4
         London. 1718. 8vo.
2nd ed.   ,,   1718. 8vo.
3rd ed.   ,,   1719. 8vo.

EVELYN (John). Sylva, or, a discourse of forest trees, &c. . 65
3rd pt.   London. 1664. Fol.
3rd ed.   ,,   1679. Fol.
5th ed.   ,,   1729. Fol.
Another ed.   York.   1776. 4to.
  ,,   ,,   2 vols.   ,,   1786. 4to.
3rd   ,,   ,,   ,,   1801. 4to.
4th   ,,   ,,   ,,   1812. 4to.

  PAGE

FELTON (Samuel). Miscellanies on Ancient and Modern Gardening, and on the Scenery of Nature. London. 1785. 8vo. viii

FELTON (Samuel). On the Portraits of English Authors on Gardening. vii
        London. 1828. 8vo.
2nd ed.   ,,   1830. 8vo.

FITZ-STEPHEN (G.). [*See*] Stephanides (G.) 21

G., R. British Topography. [By R. G., *i.e.* R. Gough]. . 9
London. 1780. 4to.

GARDENER'S LABYRINTH. [*See*] Mountain (D.) . . . 2

GARDENER'S MAGAZINE. 19 vols. London. 1826-1843. 8vo. v. & 73
[Oct. 1826, and Jan. 1827 referred to.]

GERARD (John). The Herball, or generall historie of plantes 2
        London. 1597. Fol.
Another ed.   ,,   1633. Fol.

GOOGE (Barnaby). [*See*] Heresbach (Conrad) . . 83

GOUGH (R.). [*See*] G., R. 9

HAMPTON COURT, Five Views of. By Highmore; engraved by Tinney. 4

HAMPTON COURT AND ITS GARDENS. Published by Wilkinson 8

HAMPTON COURT. Plan of the Royal Palace and Gardens of Hampton Court, by Rocque. 1736. 8

HAMPTON COURT. A View of the Gardens of Hampton Court, by Mannskirch; engraved by Schutz. 1798. . . . 8

HARLEIAN MANUSCRIPT, No. 5308. Variety of Plans for Garden Plots, Wildernesses, &c. Neatly drawn on paper, but without any writing at all 2

BIBLIOGRAPHY.

HERESBACH (Conrad). Foure Bookes of Husbandry... Newely Englished, and increased by Barnaby Googe. . . . 83
London. 1577. 4to.
Another ed.   ,,   1578. 4to.
  ,,   ,,   ,,   1586. 4to.
  ,,   ,,   ,,   1601. 4to.
  ,,   ,,   ,,   1614. 4to.
  ,,   ,,   ,,   1631. 4to.

HIGHMORE ( ). [*See*] Hampton Court 4

HIRSCHFELD (Christian Cayus Lorenz). Theorie der Gardenkunst 60
Leipsig. 1775. 8vo.
Another ed. 2 vols.   ,,   1779–85. 4to.

HIRSCHFELD (Christian Cayus Lorenz). Theorie de l'art des Jardins, ... traduit de l'Allemand, &c. 60
5 tom. Leipsig. 1779–85. 4to.

HONINGTON HALL. View of Honington Hall, in the county of Warwick, the seat of Sir Henry Parker, Bart., by Buck. 1731. 4

HUTCHINS (John). History and Antiquities of the county of Dorset. Second ed. corrected, &c. (By R. Gough and J. B. Nichols.) 4 vols. London. 1796–1815. Fol. . . . 88
1st ed. 2 vols. London. 1774. Fol.
3rd ,, 4 vols. Westminster. 1861–73. Fol.

JACOB (Giles). The Country Gentleman's Vade mecum . . 4
London. 1717. 12mo.

JAMES (John). The theory and practice of Gardening ... done from the French [of J. B. A. Le Blond]. By J. J. . 4
London. 1712. 4to.

KEITH (Patrick). System of Physiological Botany . . . viii
2 vols. London. 1816. 8vo.

KENNET (White). Parochial Antiquities attempted in the history of Ambrosden, Burcester, ... in the counties of Oxford and Bucks. 3
Oxford. 1695. 4to.
Another ed. 2 vols.   ,,   1818. 4to.

BIBLIOGRAPHY.

                                                             PAGE

KENT. Thirty-six views of Noblemen and Gentlemen's seats in the county of Kent, all designed upon the spot, by T. Badeslade. Fol. 7

KENT (Nathaniel). General View of the Agriculture of the County of Norfolk. 1794. 4to. . . . . 22 & 23

KNIGHT (R. P.). A Review of The Landscape, also of an Essay [by Sir U. Price] on the Picturesque. London. 1795. 4to. 27

LANGLEY (Batty). New Principles of Gardening . . . 4
London. 1728. 4to.

LA QUINTINIE (J. de). Compleat Gard'ner . . . Abridg'd . . .
by G. London and Henry Wise 3
              London. 1699. 8vo.
Another ed.   ,,   1704. 8vo.
  ,,   ,,   ,,   1710. 8vo.

LAWRENCE (John) or LAURENCE. Clergyman's Recreation. . 4
            London. 1714. 8vo.
3rd ed.   ,,   1715. 8vo.
4th ed.   ,,   1716. 8vo.
5th ed.   ,,   1717. 8vo.
6th ed.   ,,   1726. 8vo.

LELAND (John). The Itinerary of John Leland the Antiquary, publish'd . . . by T. Hearne. 8
      9 vols. Oxford. 1710-12. 8vo. Vol. 8 in 2 pt.
2nd ed.   ,,   ,,   1745-44. 8vo.
3rd ed.   ,,   ,,   1770. 8vo.

LOGGAN (David). Cantabrigia illustrata. Cantabrigiæ. [1688.] Fol. 5

LOGGAN (David). Oxonia illustrata. Oxoniæ. 1765. Fol. . 5

LONDON, View of. 1563. [See] also Pennant's London . . 23

LONDON (George). Compleat Gard'ner 3
[See] La Quintinie (J. de).

BIBLIOGRAPHY.

	PAGE
LONDON (George) and WISE (Henry). Retir'd Gard'ner	3
2 vols. London. 1706. 8vo.	
2nd ed. ,, 1717. 8vo.	
LOUDON or LAUDON (Gideon Ernst)	69
[*See*] Pezzl (Johann). La vie du Feldmaréchal Baron de Loudon, &c.	
LOUDON (John Claudius). An Encyclopædia of Gardening.	vi & 1
London. 1822. 8vo.	
Another ed. ,, 1835. 8vo.	
,, ,, ,, 1850. 8vo.	
LYLE. Herbal	15
LYSONS (Daniel). The Environs of London.	9
4 vols. London. 1792-96. 4to.	
Supp. to 1st ed. ,, 1811. 4to.	
2nd ed. of 'Environs.' 2 vols. ,, 1811. 4to.	
LYSONS (Daniel) and (Samuel). Magna Britannia; Vol. 1-6 containing Bedford, Berks, Bucks; Cambridgeshire and Cheshire; Cornwall, Cumberland, Derby and Devon. London. [1806]-22. 4to. [Published in parts.]	9 & 12
MAGNA BRITANNIA. [*See*] Lysons (D.) and (S.)	9 & 12
MALONE ( ). [*See*] Aubrey (J.) Lives of Eminent Men.	14
MAVOR (W.). [*See*] Tusser (Thomas)	77
MERCIER (B.). Funeral Oration of a Peasant.	79
MILLER (Philip). The Gardener's Dictionary	4
2 vols. London. 1731. Fol.	
2nd ed. ,, 1733. Fol.	
3rd ed. ,, 1737. Fol.	
6th ed. ,, 1752. Fol.	
9th ed. ,, 1835-6. 8vo.	
THE MIRROR. (No. 311 referred to.) London. 1823-49. 8vo. 4 Series. 53 vols.	xi
MORANT (Philip). History and Antiquities of the County of Essex. 2 vols. London. 1768. Fol.	6

	PAGE
MOUNTAIN (Didymus) [*i.e.* Thomas Hill]. The Gardener's Labyrinth. Completed by H. Dethick . . . . 2 pt. London. 1577. 4to.	2
,, 1594. 4to.	
,, 1594. 4to.	
,, 1652. 4to.	
,, 1656. 4to.	

MULLER ( ). [*See*] Vauxhall 8

NOURSE (Timothy). Campania Fælix; or, a Discourse of the
benefits and improvements of Husbandry 4
London. 1700. 8vo.
2nd ed. ,, 1706. 8vo.

OXFORD ALMANACKS. Oxford. 1673-17—? 8vo. . . . 9

PECK (Francis). Desiderata Curiosa 11
2 vols. London. 1732. Fol.
New ed. ,, ,, 1779. 4to.

PENNANT (Thomas). Of London 23
London. 1790. 4to.
2nd ed. ,, 1791. 4to.
3rd ed. Dublin 1791. 8vo.
Another ed. London. 1793. 4to.
4th ed. ,, 1805. 4to.
*5th ed. ,, 1813. 8vo.

PEZZL (Johann). La vie du Feldmaréchal Baron de Loudon,
traduite de l'Allemand . . . par le Baron de Bock . . 69
Luxemburg. 1792. 12mo.

PLOT (Robert) Dr. Natural History of Oxfordshire . . 9
Oxford. [1677.] Fol. Plates by M. Burgher.
2nd ed., with additions. Oxford. 1705. Fol.

POPE (Alexander). Letters of Mr. Pope 88
2 vols. London. 1735. 8vo.
[Several editions of these 'Letters' were pub. in 1735.]

PRICE (Sir Uvedale) 27
[*See*] Knight (R. P.). A Review of the Landscape, &c. 1795.

* 5th edition called 'Some account of London.'

BIBLIOGRAPHY.

	PAGE
PRICE (Sir Uvedale). An Essay on the Picturesque . . .	2
2 vols. London. 1794–98. 8vo.	
Another ed. ,, 1796–98. 8vo.	
,, ,, 3 vols. ,, 1810. 8vo.	
,, ,, Edinburgh. 1842. 8vo.	

PRICE (Sir Uvedale). A Letter to H. Repton . . . on the application of the practice as well as the principles of landscape-painting to landscape-gardening, intended as a supplement to the Essays on the Picturesque . . . 27
London. 1795. 8vo.

PULTENEY (Richard). Historical and Biographical Sketches of the Progress of Botany in England. London. 1790. 8v. vii & x

RALEIGH (Sir Walter), Remaines of. London. 1675. 24mo. 89
[This work contains the 'Letter to his wife' referred to on p. 89.]

RAY (John). Catalogus Plantarum Angliæ vi
  Londini. 1670. 8vo.
Editio secunda.   ,,   1677. 8vo.

RAY (John). Historia Plantarum. Londini. 1686–1704. Fol. vi

RIGAUD (   ). [See] Stowe, co. Bucks. A general plan, &c. . 8

RODD (Horatio). Catalogue of authentic portraits, painted in oil, on pannel and canvas, miniatures, &c. . . . 10
London. 1824. 4to.

RYSBRAKE [See] Chiswick. Two Views, &c. . . .

ST. JOHN (Hector). [See] Crèvecœur (M. G. J. de) . . . viii

SHAKESPEARE (William). Cymbeline . . . . 21 & 22
  London. 1784. 8vo.
Another ed.   ,,   1795. 8vo.
,,   ,,   ,,   1815. 8vo.
,,   ,,   ,,   1872. 8vo.
,,   ,,   ,,   1881. 8vo.
,,   ,,   ,,   1886. 8vo.
,,   ,,   ,,   1889. 8vo.

I

BIBLIOGRAPHY.

				PAGE
SHAKESPEARE (William).	Love's Labour Lost.			21 & 22
	London.	1598.	8vo.	
Another ed.	,,	1631.	8vo.	
,, ,,	,,	1777.	8vo.	
,, ,,	,,	1839.	8vo.	
,, ,,	,,	1862.	8vo.	
,, ,,	,,	1873.	8vo.	

SHAW (Stebbing). A Tour to the West of England in 1788. . 12
    London. 1789. 8vo.
    Ano. ed. ,, 1798. 8vo. Mavor's Brit. Tourists. Vol. 4.
    ,, ,, ,, 1808. 8vo. Pinkerton's Voyages. Vol. 2.
    ,, ,, ,, 1809. 12mo. Mavor's Brit. Tourists. Vol. 3.

SHERARD (James), Dr. Garden at Eltham 24
    [*See*] Dillenius (J. J.) Hortus Elthamensis, &c.

SKELTON (Joseph). Oxonia Antiqua Restaurata. . . 5
    2 vols. Oxford. 1823. 4to.

SOUTHGATE (Richard). Catalogue of Pictures. 1826. . . 10

STAINBOROUGH, co. Yorkshire. A view of Stainborough and Wentworth Castle in the county of York, one of the Seats of the Earl of Strafford, by Badeslade, engraved by Harris. 1730. 8

STEPHANIDES (Gulielmus). Fitz-Stephen's description of the City of London, newly translated from the Latin original . . . . [by S. Pegge.] Lat. and Eng. London. 1772. 4to. 21

STEPHANIDES (Gulielmus). Descriptio nobilissimæ civitatis Londoniæ 21
    [*See*] Stow (John). Survey of London, &c. 1598 ed.
                           ,, ,, 1603 ,,
        Leland (J.). The Itinerary. Vol. 8. 1745 ,,
                           ,, ,, 1770 ,,

STEVENSON (Henry). The Young Gardner's Director, &c. . 4
    London. 1716. 12mo.
    5th ed. Gentleman Gardener instructed, &c.
        London. 1764. 12mo.
    8th ed. ,, 1769. 12mo.

BIBLIOGRAPHY. 115

Stow (John). Survey of London 58
  London. 1598. Fol.
  Another ed. „ 1603. „
  Last „ „ 1893. 8vo.

Stowe, co. Bucks. A general Plan of the Woods, Park, and Gardens of Stowe, the Seat of Lord Cobham, with three large and twelve small Views in the Gardens, by Rigaud and Baron; published by Sarah Bridgeman. 1739. Fol. . 8

Stowe, co. Bucks. Sixteen perspective Views, with a general Plan of the Buildings and Gardens at Stow, in the County of Bucks, belonging to Earl Temple, drawn on the spot by M. Chatelain, 1752; engraved by G. Bickham, jun. . . 8
Oblong. Fol.

Stukeley (William). Itinerarium curiosum, &c. . . .
  London. 1724 Fol.
  2nd ed. 2 pt. „ 1776 „

Switzer (Stephen). Ichnographia, or the nobleman, gentleman, and gardener's recreation 4
  London. 1718. 8vo.
  3 vols. „ 1741-42. „

Switzer (Stephen). An introduction to a general system of hydrostaticks and hydraulicks, &c. 4
  2 vols. London. 1729. 4to.

Switzer (Stephen). The practical fruit gardener, &c. . . 4
  London. 1724. 8vo.
  2nd ed. „ 1731. ,
  Another copy „ 1752. ,
  [The last has a different title-page.

Temple (Sir William). Gardens of Epicurus 1
  [See] Temple's Works.

Temple (Sir William). Works of 17
  2 vols. London. 1720. Fol
  „ „ 1731. ,
  „ „ 1750. , ·

TEMPLE (Sir William). Works of *(continued)*—
4 vols. Edinburgh. 1754. 8vo.
,, London 1757. ,,
,, ,, 1770. ,,
,, ,, 1814. ,,

TICKELL (Thomas). [*See*] Addison (J.) Rt. Hon. Works, &c. 16

TINNEY ( ). [*See*] Hampton Court 4

THE TOPOGRAPHER 12
4 vols. London. 1789-91. 8vo.
Another ed. ,, 1791. 4to.
[Vol IV. only. With plates of Vols. I.-III., with letterpress as are necessary to their illustrations.]

TOUNSON (Robert). A letter relating to the last behaviour of Sir Walter Rawleigh, &c. 89
[*See*] Walterus, de Hemingburgh.
Vol. I. Appendix clxxxiv.-clxxxvi.

TUSSER (Thomas). Five hundreth points of good husbandry vnited to as many of good huswiferie, &c. 77
New ed. with notes . . . by W. Mavor.
London. 1812. 4to.
Another ed. Oxford. 1848. 16mo.
Last ed., published by the English Dialect Society.
London. 1878. 8vo.

VAUXHALL. A general Prospect of Vauxhall Gardens, shewing at one View the disposition of the whole Gardens, by Wale; engraved by Muller. 1751 8

VERTUE'S WALPOLE. [*See*] Walpole (Horace) vii

VERTUE (George). A description of the works of . . . W. Hollar 9
London. 1745. 4to.
2nd ed. ,, 1759. ,

WALE ( ). [*See*] Vauxhall . . . . . .

BIBLIOGRAPHY.

WALPOLE (Horace), Earl of Orford. Anecdotes of Painting in England, . . . Collected by G. Vertue, &c. . . vii & 21
    4 vols. Strawberry Hill. 1762–71. 4to.
 2nd ed. ,, ,, ,, 1765–71. ,,
 3rd ,, ,, London 1782. 8vo.
 4th ,, 5 vols. ,, 1786. ,,
 *Another ed. ,, ,, 1826–28. ,,
 New ,, 3 vols. ,, 1849. ,,
 Another ,, 1 vol. ,, 1879. ,,
 ,, ,, 3 vols. ,, 1888. ,,

WALTERUS, DE HEMINGBURGH. Walteri Hemingford . . . Historia de rebus gestis Edvardi I., II., III. Publicavit, T. Hearnius 89
 2 vols. Oxoniæ. 1731. 8vo.

WARTON (Thomas). History of English Poetry . . . 22
    4 vols. London. 1774–81. 8vo.
 2nd ed. 3 ,, ,, 1775–81. ,,
 Another ed. 4 ,, ,, 1824 ,,
 ,, 3 ,, ,, 1840 ,,
 ,, 4 ,, ,, 1871 ,,

WILLIAMS (William). Oxonia depicta 5
 [Oxford. 1732–3.] Fol.

WILTON, in Wiltshire. An exact Plan of the Gardens and Park at Wilton; the Seat of Henry, Earl of Pembroke, together with the Town; also Plans and Views of some of the Buildings in the gardens; by J. Rocque. 1746 . . 7

WISE (Henry). Compleat Gard'ner 3
 [*See*] La Quintinie (J. de).

WISE (Henry), and LONDON (George). Retir'd Gard'ner . . 3
 2 vols. London. 1716. 8vo.
 2nd ed. ,, 1717. ,,

WITHERS (William). Letter to Sir W. Scott, Bart., respecting certain . . . errors in his late essay on Planting, &c. . 22 & 78
 London. 1828. 8vo.

 * This edition, edited by the Rev. J. Dallaway, is the one referred to.

THE WORLD. No. 118. (1755) referred to	17

    4 vols. London. [1753–56]. Fol.
  Another ed. 6 ,,   ,,   1755–57. 12mo.
  3rd ed.   4 ,,   ,,   1761.   ,,
  And numerous other editions.

WORLIDGE (John). Systema Agriculturæ, &c.	9

  London. 1669. Fol.
    ,,   1677. ,,
    ,,   1681. ,,
    ,,   1697. 8vo.
    ,,   1716. ,,

WORLIDGE (John). Systema Horticulturæ; or, the Art of Gardening	viii & 3

        London. 1677. 8vo.
  Another ed.   ,,   1683. ,,
    ,,   ,,   1688. ,,

INDEX.

Albury, Vineyard of, 9
Alloway, Gardens of, 53, 54
—— Views from, 54
Althorp, 16, 47
Alton Grove, near Nottingham, 26
Ananas, an Indian Fruit, 14
Andernach, Wine from, 86
Anderson, Sir Edmund, 15
Anne, Queen, 1
Aristotle, 64
Arlington, Lord, 29
Arundel, Lord, 9
Arviragus, 67
Ashmolean Museum, 9
Ashridge. 30
—— Abbey, 12
Aspeden Hall, 2, 3
Athens, 5
—— Gardens in, 83
Athol, Duke of, 53
Audley End, 15

Bacchus, 99
Backrach, Wine from, 86
Bacon, Lord, 14
Balgony. 54
Balle, Mr., Garden at Campden House, 20
Baltimore, Lord, 38
Barclay, Earl of, 37
'Bard of Twickenham,' The, 99
Barker, Mr., 35
Barleduke, Wine of, 86
Bateman, Sir James, 38
Beau-lieu, House called, 29
Beddington, Gardens of, 15, 88
Bedford, Countess of, 17
—— House, 39
Bedfordshire, 40
Bellucci, 43, 44
Bienheim, 24
Blount, Martha, Letter from Pope, 17, 88

Boileau's Epitaph on Racine, 6
Bolton, Duke of, 16
Boscobel Garden, 9
Bossuet, 82
Boucher, 33
Boughton, 16, 17
Box-tree Hedge, 20
Bradford, Earl of, 33
Braithwaite, Mr., 18
Bratby, 48
Bretby Park, 25
Brewood, 15
Bridges, Mr. Paymaster-General, 41
Bridgewater Archives, 12
—— Duke of, 30
Bristol, Earl of, 90
Brooke, Lady, Garden at Hackney, 16
—— Lord, 33
Buckingham, Murder of, 13
Burges, Wine from, 86
Burlington Palace, 40
Burns, on Burial of, 67
Bushey Park, 33
Byers, Justice, 32
Byfronts, Mr. Taylor's Garden at, 36

Cambridge, 39
—— Gardens at, 5
—— R. O., 17
Camelford, Lord, 62
—— Lord, Burial-place of, 60
Campden House, 20
Cannons, 16, 41
Canterbury, 36
Capel, Lord, 35
Cardigan, Earl of, Seat near Reading, 30
Carew, Sir N., Gardens of, 88
Carews, Seat of the, 15
Carleton, Lord, Seat of, 31

INDEX.

Northumberland House, 39
Nottingham, 48

Orford, Lady, Garden in Dorsetshire, 17
Orleans, Wine from, 86
Oxford, Gardens of, 5, 46
Oxnead Hall, 1
Oxton House, Devon, 27

Pargotti, 44
Parham Downs, Sir B. Dixwel's Garden at, 36
Paris, Wine of, 86
Penmure, Earl of, 51
—— Palace of, 52
Pentre, Pembroke, 27
Peterborough, Earl of, 39
Petrarch, 75
Physic Gardens at Oxford, 19
Picturesque, Writer on, 1
Pitfour, 58
Platt, Sir Hugh, 14
Pompadour, Madame de, 24
Pope, A., Bust of, 99
—— Letter to Martha Blount, 88
—— Pope's Mother, Obelisk to her Memory, 101
—— Villa at Twickenham, 96
Portland, Duke of, 31
Powis Castle, 27
Price, Sir Uvedale, 2
—— Letter to Mr. Repton, 27
Prior Park, 8
Privy Gardens, 23
Pruning, Improper, 22, 23
Putney, 39

Queenhithe, Garden opposite, 23
Quintinie, Mr., 47

Racine, Epitaph on, 6
Raleigh, Sir W., Execution of, 89
—— Garden of, 88
—— Wife of, 88
Repton, Mr., 27
Richard (Garrick's), 21
Richardson, Samuel, 19
Richmond, 31
—— Green, 14, 32
Rochester, Earl of, 16
—— —— Gardens of, 31
Rosalyn, Abbey of, 58
Rousham, 18
Rubens, Tapestry of, 91
Russell, Lord William, 18

Russia, Empress of, her Garden at St. Petersburg, 99

St. Germains, Gardens of, 27
St. Helen's, Bishopsgate Street, 21
St. Just, Curious Garden at, 26
Salisbury, 46
—— House, 39
Saresden House, 3
Savoy, The, 39
Saxe-Gotha, Duke of, 61
Scarbrough, Earl of, 16, 37
Scawen, Sir W., 37
Schuykill, River, 67
Scotch Gardens, Account of some, 28
Scott, Sir W., Letter from W. Withers, 78
Scudamore, Viscount, 13
Seaton, 50
Shakespeare, W., Attachment to Botany, 22
—— Quotation from, 96
Sherard, Dr., 24
Sherborn, 46
Sherborne, Account of, 88
Shirley, Hon. Mr., 96
Sion House, 14
Skipworth, Thomas, 34
Somerset, Duke of, 14
—— House, 39
Stainborough House, 8
Stanhope, Sir William, 97
—— Bust of, 100
—— Bust of his Daughter, 100
Stanstead, 16, 17
Stanton Harold, 48
Sterne, 75
Stowe, Gardens at, 8
Strafford, Earl of, 33, 34
Strand Gardens, 23
Stratton, 18
Stukeley, William, Portrait of, 10
Sunderland, Earl of, 16
Sutton Court, 35
Swift's Lord Cork, 6
Switzer, Designer of Leeswood Garden, 27
Sydney, Sir Philip, Portrait of, 9

Tallard, Marshal, 48
—— —— Garden at Nottingham, 3
Temple, Sir William, 17, 32
Terragle, 49
Theobald's Garden, 11

INDEX. 123

Theobald's Park, 24
Theophrastus, 64
Thoresby Park, 26
Thrasybulus 83
Thurlow, Lord, 62
Thutteby, 48
Tooke, Horne, 62, 63
Tradescant, Portrait of, 10
Traquair, Earl of, 49
——— Palace of, 49
Troy House, near Monmouth, 25
Tunbridge Wells, 36
Turner, Dr., Garden at Wells, 14
Tweeddale, Marquis of, 50
Twickenham, 33
Tyrtaine, 64

Uborn, 30

Vauxhall, Gardens at, 8
Villiams, Lord, of Tame, 86
Villiers, Seat of the, 36
Vine, Cultivation of the, 85
——— ——— in England, 83
Voltaire, 75

Wales, Curious Custom of, 66
Walpole, Horace, 2
Wanstead, 29
Ward, Mr., 38
Ware Park, 12
Warton, Dr. Thomas, 5
Watson, Dr., Bishop of Llandaff, 74
Weeping Willow, Celebrated, 99
Westerham, Garden at, 11

West Wycombe, 8
Whitehall, 39
Whitton, 8
Wickart, Dr., 18
William III., 1
Wilson, the Ornithologist, 67
Wilton Gardens, 7, 8
Wimbledon, 38
Winchenden, 30
Winchester, 45
——— Garden near, 18
Windsor, Fair at, in Henry V.'s reign, 21
Wines, On, 85, 86, 87
Winton, 51
——— Lord, 51
Witham, General, 36
Withers, W., Letter to Sir W. Scott, 78
Woodhouselee, near Roslin, 28
Wootton, 3
Worcester House, 39
Worlidge, On the Attachment for Gardens, 73
Wotton, Sir H., 12
Wresehill Castle, 21
Wrest, 16

Yester, 50
Yew Tree, The, 19
——— Trees of Hillingdon, 19
York House, 39
Young, 3

Zucchero, 9

www.ingramcontent.com/pod-product-compliance
Lightning Source LLC
Chambersburg PA
CBHW030900170426
43193CB00009BA/686